TONGUES
Dissecting the Gift

by
Teresita Pérez

TEACH Services, Inc.
P U B L I S H I N G
www.TEACHServices.com • (800) 367-1844

World rights reserved. This book or any portion thereof may not be copied or reproduced in any form or manner whatever, except as provided by law, without the written permission of the publisher, except by a reviewer who may quote brief passages in a review.

This book was written to provide truthful information in regard to the subject matter covered. The author assumes full responsibility for the accuracy of all facts and quotations as cited in this book. The opinions expressed in this book are the author's personal views and interpretation of the Bible, Spirit of Prophecy, and/or contemporary authors and do not necessarily reflect those of TEACH Services, Inc.

This book is sold with the understanding that the publisher is not engaged in giving spiritual, legal, medical, or other professional advice. If authoritative advice is needed, the reader should seek the counsel of a competent professional

---

Copyright © 2004, 2013 TEACH Services, Inc.
ISBN-13: 978-1-57258-832-5 (Paperback)
ISBN-13: 978-1-57258-833-2 (ePub)
ISBN-13: 978-1-57258-834-9 (Kindle / Mobi)
Library of Congress Control Number: 2013932411

All scripture quotations, unless otherwise indicated, are taken from the King James Version Bible.

Scripture quotations marked "NKJV™" are taken from the New King James Version®. Copyright © 1982 by Thomas Nelson, Inc. Used by permission. All rights reserved.

All scripture quotations, unless otherwise indicated, are taken from the Holy Bible, New International Version®, NIV®. Copyright ©1973, 1978, 1984 by Biblica, Inc.™ Used by permission of Zondervan. All rights reserved worldwide.

Published by

www.TEACHServices.com • (800) 367-1844

Preface

As Christians, we have witnessed the role of the Trinity in the salvation of humankind. In the Old Testament, the Father led the people of Israel to the promised land. They could talk to him face to face. A redeemer was to be born—the Son of Man. As was promised in Genesis. 3:15, that seed was Jesus Christ who would come to save humanity. Once again people would be able to talk to Him face to face. He was made flesh and dwelt among us.

As Jesus ascended to Heaven He promised the participation of the third member of the Trinity—The Holy Spirit. He would be the "Parakletos," the one who would walk side by side with us, helping us to comprehend the great gift of salvation and how to apply it to our lives. We live in the era of the Spirit. He was seen in full power by the disciples. After taking over the assignment given by Jesus, they received the power of the Holy Spirit to accomplish the mission of reaching out with the gospel of salvation.

This gift given to man has been misunderstood. Jesus told His disciples that He would abide with them through the Spirit. The purpose of the Spirit was to come into our hearts and start the work of regeneration and transformation in our lives. The tongues of fire were seen as the power from above, bestowed upon His chosen ones, for a special task.

Many religions have arisen because people do not understand the Scriptures and the role of the Holy Spirit. There are those who want to live in the Age of the Father and the Old Testament is their rule of faith. Others reject the Old Testament and base their faith in the New Testament. Then there are those who want to live with just the Spirit! Supernatural manifestations are their main emphasis.

We must understand the whole Bible! God the Father, God the Son and God the Holy Spirit are active in the salvation of each one of us. The Bible talks about another time when we shall see the Spirit in full power at the end of time. **TONGUES** *Dissecting the Gift* gives us an excellent picture of the work of the Holy Spirit then, now and at that future time. It analyzes in a succinct format the whole scope of the Bible, with special emphasis in the Holy Spirit. Let us put ourselves at His disposition, like the apostles, that we may be led by the Spirit.

Pr. Leo S. Ranzolin

My deepest gratitude to my husband and my sons, my sister, and my friend, Karin Alderfer, for encouraging me to publish this work. I also thank many others who took time to proofread and/or listen to my exposition of this subject when I first began to share it. In no particular order, they are Daniel and Mabel Jimenez, Jorge Benavides, Fernando and Norka Munilla, Pr. Gerardo Brito, Pr. Fernando Paulín, Pr. Salim Japas (1921-1992) and Pr. Robert Boggess. In particular I wish to express profound gratitude to Pr. Leo Ranzolin for taking time from his very busy schedule to read this study and grace it with its preface.

Teresita Pérez

TABLE OF CONTENTS

Background vii
1   Tower of Babel 9
2   Pentecost 12
3   Cornelius, A Gentile 23
4   Ephesus 30
5   Corinth 35
6   Dissecting the Gift 41
7   Corinth Repents 49
8   Words Good and True 60
9   Interpretation 67
10   Miracles 72
11   Prove Those in Ministry 80
12   Casting Out Demons 90
13   Love and Tongues 93
14   Women at Corinth 109
15   The Latter Rain 118
Testimony 138
Poem: Righteous By Faith 141

BACKGROUND

We are living in the eve of Armageddon. Is it possible that in times like these when the world needs clear messages of guidance and warning, that God would cause His people to speak such that they themselves do not even know what they are saying? Determined to find the answer to that question, I embarked in a research so intense and detailed, that at one point, after having seen me for many months studying and taking notes daily many hours at a time, and oftentimes throughout the night, my husband asked me, "Are you copying the Bible by hand?" This book is the product of that extensive research.

It seemed to me that since Satan tried to duplicate the first coming of Christ prior to Jesus' birth, (Acts 5:34-39) and we have been warned that in the last days he will surely deceive, if possible, even the very elect, (Matthew 24:24) that it would be prudent to earnestly study the gift of tongues to ascertain its veracity. There had to be a way of knowing, when someone spoke in tongues, whether it was God's gift or a counterfeit. But how could one distinguish between the two? Taking someone's word for it was not good enough. In fact, the apostle Paul himself pointed out that a group of Christians who listened earnestly to his and Silas' teachings did not simply take their words at face value. Rather, they examined the Scriptures daily to see whether those teachings were in harmony with God's Word. Paul complimented those who questioned even him, and declared them to be nobler than those who did not question what they were told. (Acts 17:10-11) In like manner, it would be wise of the reader to also diligently search the Scriptures to analyze and dissect the subject of tongues, and understand for yourself whether these things that you will read here are so.

Sometime after I commenced sharing my findings, at a study I was presenting, I had not spoken yet for fifteen minutes when a woman who was perhaps in her late 50's became furious. It turned out that she was a pastor's wife and challenged me asking whether I had checked the book *Acts of the Apostles*, by E.G. White, when arriving at my conclusions, because, she contended, they contradicted what was exposed in that book. I answered, "No." For, truthfully, I had armed myself only with a Bible and a concordance. Thereupon she gave me that book and ordered me to read aloud. I submitted to her wishes. And, to my amazement, the very first cite I read was in agreement with my own conclusions. I looked up at the pastor's wife and she was livid. She snatched the book from my hands and read the words herself. The argument she provoked was thus settled, though her resentment remained stamped on her face.

It was an awful experience which served a good objective: It caused me to review the White writings on this subject. Therefore, in order to assist interested readers, some of the footnotes in this book are the E.G. White cites derived from my subsequent research.

May God richly bless you and His Spirit give you discernment as you study this material.

Teresita Pérez

Note: Throughout this book all emphasis is mine unless otherwise noted.

1

TOWER OF BABEL

God instructed the sons of Noah to fill the earth. (Genesis 9:1) Instead, they chose a common area wherein to dwell together and build a tower. (*Ibid.,* 11:1-6) God then interfered with what they, in defiance to His command, proposed to do and caused them to misunderstand each other by confusing their tongue. (vs. 7) The apparent babel in speech sealed the site as the *Tower of Babel*.

The action of interrupting their work by creating language barriers between different groups caused Noah's descendants to separate from each other. Consequently they migrated to different areas, "every one after his tongue," (Genesis 10:5, 20, 31) just as God had purposed for them to do in the first place. (vs. 11:8-9)

Technologically speaking we could say that God removed, uninstalled, took away from each individual the *common-language program* originally existing in the "computer" of their mind, and substituted in its place a *new-language program*, such that a different and unique *new-language* was given to a family or groups of people for them to communicate with each other in their own distinct tongue. The word "tongue" (Genesis 10:5, 20, 31) is a synonym of the word "language," (Genesis 11:1, 7, 9) and its Biblical definition is the same as the standard definition for that word: the oral structure of sounds by which means groups of people communicate intelligently with one another.

That generation had proposed to do contrary to what God commanded, but it was not so with the children of Israel. When God gave His Law and statutes, the Israelites exclaimed, "All that the

Lord hath said will we do, and be obedient." (Exodus 24:7) It was a promise they determined to keep. Yet, though their intentions were well-meaning, man cannot obey God merely by human effort. Thus the Israelites' story is the same as ours, for in the power of the flesh is revealed that we are continually engaged in never-ending disobedience. Such was also Paul's spiritual battle. (Romans 7:14-25) Hence the admonition given that we are to pray and not faint, pray always, pray without ceasing, and remain always, continually attached to the True Vine. (Luke 18:1; 21:36; 1 Thessalonians 5:17; John 15:1-8)

But the remnant of Israel did carry on God's work and we have them to thank for the New Testament. Yet they did not assert a promise, but instead prayed for God's promise of His Spirit, and when the Holy Spirit was given to them, they accomplished the vast work of evangelizing such that they turned the world upside down. (Acts 17:6) They preached in other tongues, other languages, because, without removing their *native-language program*, a *second-language program* was "installed" in them; that is, they received the gift of a new tongue for each of them to speak, so that now, in addition to their mother tongue, each disciple became a fully bilingual, or perhaps multilingual, individual.[1]

Their message was salvation in a resurrected Savior. It revealed the Creator's Son, submissive and docile, surrendering to the will of men to put Him to death, when all He wanted was for them to surrender to His Father's will that He may give them eternal life. Israel's remnant carried out the order entrusted to them to "go into all the world." (Matthew 28:19; Mark 16:15) The miracle bestowed upon them which first appeared on Pentecost, is commonly known as "speaking in tongues," and is recorded in Scripture four times:

1. On the day Pentecost, (Acts 2)

---

[1] "From this time forth the language of the disciples was pure, simple, and accurate, whether they spoke in their native tongue or in a foreign language." (*Acts of the Apostles*, p. 40)

2. In the home of Cornelius, (Acts 10 and 11)
3. At Ephesus, (Acts 19:1-6) and
4. At Corinth. (1 Corinthians 14)

We will proceed to consider each of those passages.

2

PENTECOST

The first time the promised gift of the Holy Spirit was poured out to the Christian church was at Jerusalem on the day of Pentecost, a feast that attracted Jews from every land and who did not speak the language of that city. On that day, about one-hundred-and-twenty disciples were gathered behind closed doors, at a time in history when they feared for their lives. They were all praying and were as one man in their belief. Then a sudden sound as of rushing wind came out of heaven and bid them go out to preach to the visitors at Jerusalem, speaking in tongues. (Acts 2:1-12) They preached salvation in Jesus resurrected and, as a result, about three-thousand souls were added to the group of believers that same day, (vs. 2:36-40) and many more daily. (vs. 2:41, 4:4)

Jesus had instructed: "Go ye therefore, and teach all nations...." (Matthew 28:19; Mark 16:15) But how could a group of scared persons, voluntarily locked-in, go to preach to every nation? Yet they had a message to give and a place wherein to give it. The message was salvation in Jesus resurrected, and the place was the whole world, wherein Jerusalem would be the starting point. Additionally, the language barrier presented an obstruction to their work. Therefore, *both* the compelling power of God, so they would not fear and those who listened would be impacted by their teaching, *and* the gift of tongues, were necessary for Christianity to spread at all, and both were supplied when the Holy Spirit was gifted to them as promised.

Let us now define the difference between a disciple and an

apostle. Disciples are the multitude of believers, (Acts 6:2, 6) and they are always growing in number. (vs. 7) We are all disciples. However, among all of the disciples of the Lord, there were twelve who were unique because they were *personally* chosen by Jesus. Those twelve men who were individually set apart by Christ Himself are called apostles. And both terms, disciples and apostles, could be used when we refer to the twelve, whereas the rest of those who are Jesus' followers, including us, are referred to only as disciples.

On the day of Pentecost the Holy Spirit was imparted to *all* of the 120 *disciples* gathered, (vs. 1-4) removed their fear and entrusted them with the ability to speak foreign languages, previously unknown to them but now new to them. The vicinities from which came the visitors to Jerusalem on the day of Pentecost were numerous and included: Parthia, Mede, Elamite, Mesopotamia, Judea, Cappadocia, Pontus, Asia, Phrygia, Pamphylia, Egypt, Libya, Cyrene, Rome, Crete, and Arabia. (Acts 2:9-11) Of these sixteen areas, in a number of them, like Judea, Mesopotamia, Arabia, Asia and others, more than one tongue was spoken. (John 19:17; Act 1:19) Therefore, there were many, many tongues represented and many disciples were needed to cover all the languages present. Perhaps groups of two, three or more disciples among the 120 were gifted with the same foreign language because they were needed to reach larger crowds of visitors from a given region. And thus it was how they who heard understood the message of the day, as each distinctive company of foreigners who shared the same mother tongue was entrusted to a different disciple.

Peter explained, "this is that which was spoken by the prophet Joel" as he referred to the Old Testament text "I will pour out my spirit... and your sons and your daughters shall prophesy...." (Acts 2:16-18; Joel 2:28-29) If both sons and daughters would prophesy, that means that both male and female disciples received the gift, for both were united as one man in their belief, in one accord. (Acts 1:14, 2:1) Perhaps there were groups of visitors formed by women only, just like us ladies tend to do to this day to chat about our own concerns, and perhaps also a few of the female disciples reached those ladies. But that assumption is only suggested as we know that all along God had used, if only sporadically mentioned, women as prophetesses and judges, such that even Israel's rulers and Levite priests sought those women for advice, guidance and God's direction. (Exodus 15:20; 2 Kings 22:14; 2 Chronicles 34:22; Nehemiah 6:14; Isaiah 8:3)However, what is being emphasized here is that dozens of languages were present and dozens of disciples, both sons and daughters as per the prophecy, were supplied to meet the need of the hour. It was a unique day, extraordinary and incomparable. It marked the dawning of the Christian era. The promised Holy Spirit officially arrived at that monumental moment in history and the work commenced with a big bang.

Did the disciples on Pentecost speak foreign tongues only that day and never again? No. The heavenly sign was not a loan, but a gift, a present, for them to keep.[2] God is very able to do that. He did it first to the folk at the Towel of Babel by giving them new tongues, and, on Pentecost God did the same but without obstructing their native tongue such that each disciple became fully bilingual or multilingual.

It was not the case that the disciples spoke their individual native tongue while the listeners heard in their own mother tongue as a result of words being miraculously translated in mid air. If you hear me address you in English, it is because I am speaking in English. Our Creator can reprogram us making us know instantly

---

2 "This miraculous gift was strong evidence to the world that their commission bore the signet of Heaven. From this time forth the language of the disciples was pure, simple, and accurate, whether they spoke in their native tongue or in a foreign language." (*Acts of the Apostles*, p. 40) And "those who understood the different languages testified to the accuracy with which these languages were used by the disciples." (*Ibid.*)

a language we did not know before. (Genesis 11) However, Satan cannot do that because he does not have the power of creation to permanently gift anyone with a real language. But God can. And He did. Moreover, that is additional proof that God can also create in us a new heart. Thus on Pentecost, the reason why the listeners understood was because the disciples were in fact speaking the languages of the visitors as God's Spirit gave the disciples "utterance." (Acts 2:4) And we have as a witness the statement of the visitors, "And how hear we every man in our own tongue, wherein we were born?" (vs. 8)[3]

God expects man to cooperate with Him as far as man is able, and then He supplies that which we have not the capability of providing. This fact is clearly presented by Jesus when he ordered men to remove the stone sealing Lazarus' tomb, because men could do that, even though Jesus could have ordered the rock itself to move out of the way and it would have obeyed. (John 11:39) However, what men could not do, that is, resurrect Lazarus, Jesus did. Likewise, on the day of Pentecost, God used, rather than angels to give His message, the disciples so that they would share their faith and knowledge of salvation in a resurrected Savior. And what the disciples lacked, the tongues in which to reach the people, was supplied by God. Thus it was that the work of evangelizing began in the joint effort of God and man. So it will always be. We choose to give our will to God, surrender in prayer to Him, and He in turn supplies our deficit by the removal of our fears filling us with peace, inception of a longing to do His good pleasure, and the power of His Spirit to perform capably whatever is necessary in accomplishing His purpose.

When Christ appeared to the two disciples on the road to Emmaus, they, not recognizing who He was, marveled that the

---

3   "[H]ere were His servants, unlettered men of Galilee, telling in all the languages then spoken, the story of His life and ministry... and those who understood the different languages testified to the accuracy with which these languages were used by the disciples." (*Acts of the Apostles*, p. 40)

stranger, Jesus, had not heard what had happened in Jerusalem with relation to Christ. So those men concluded that said stranger must have been the only person in that area ignorant of the fact that Jesus had been crucified days before. (Luke 24) That circumstance confirms that all the residents of Jerusalem already knew about what happened to Jesus. In fact, among them were the ones who rejected Him and shouted "crucify him." But the visitors, who had lost use of the language of that city, needed to be told about Christ. The message that all the residents of Jerusalem already knew, needed to be relayed by the disciples to the visitors. And the language barrier obstructing the work was conquered by the gift of tongues.

Persons who share the same language are drawn together. For example, in a tour where persons from different countries participate, groups form determined by a common language. But where do the bilinguals, like those who speak both English and Spanish, fit? They will go back and forth as conversations may interest them, but at times will also form their own group. When they do the latter, they may unconsciously mix both languages, adding Spanish words to a sentence structured for English, and vice-versa. This spontaneous ability of the brain is called "code switching" and comes with the package. Sometimes even hybrid words are created unconsciously and instantly by those of us who think in both languages. Just as you generally speak as you go, blurting out "let me sit down," or "I'll sit here," or "ah, this is a good seat," without previously taking time to decide which words to use and how to combine and structure them before you actually express yourself, so it would be if you were fully bilingual. The brain automatically draws words from its great, combined, single reservoir, structuring them without discrimination. And persons who have common vocabulary vaults find each other and form groups. So it is safe to assume that those who came to Jerusalem gathered in groups that shared the same language, not to mention that they may have known each other back home.

For the sake of comprehension, let us imagine ourselves as visitors at that time and place. Picture the thousands in Jerusalem and one of the disciples, gifted with our language, is speaking to a group forming around him. We hear our native tongue and go over to join that group, and learn from the speaker, in our own tongue, the message of salvation in a resurrected Savior.

However, let us imagine we are leaders who have already made a decision against Christ. The devil ceases the opportunity, tapping unto our intolerance and hatred, and uses us to try to obstruct and discredit the divine work. We behold those who came to partake with *us* in *our* annual feast listening in awe to those we detest. Robbed of our moment of glory, we are even blocked out of their circle because of the language barrier. Offended and enraged, our remark reveals our impotence in the face of such grand work, "These men are drunk." (Acts 2:13) Our mockery, in essence, is directed at God Himself, because pride is running our show.

Peter comes forward now to save the day. These events lead up to it: First, (starting on verse 4) we find all of the disciples speaking in tongues, "And they were all filled with the Holy Ghost, and began to speak with other tongues, as the Spirit gave them utterance." Second, (starting on verse 6) is presented the wonderment of the witnesses, "Now when this was noised abroad, the multitude came together, and were confounded, because that every man heard them speak in his own language. And they were all amazed and marvelled, saying one to another, Behold, are not all these which speak Galilaeans? And how hear we every man in our own tongue, wherein we were born?" (vs. 6-8) Third (starting on verse 13), we observe that it is those two events which trigger the mockery[4] which follows, "Others mocking said, These men are full of new wine." And fourth (starting on verse 14), the mockery, in turn, triggers Peter to confront the ridicule, "But Peter, standing up...lifted his voice and said...."

Was Peter speaking in another language to a group of visitors before addressing the mockers? Regarding Peter, it seems as if things happen in threes. Three times he denied Jesus. (Matthew 26:69-75) Three times Jesus asked Peter if he loved Him. (John 21:15-17) And also three times Peter asserts that he received the gift of tongues on Pentecost. (Acts 10 and 11) Let us look into that.

Sometime after Pentecost, Peter compared the outpouring of the Holy Spirit on that day to the phenomenon which occurred soon thereafter to Gentiles, and he made *no* distinction between the two. In what manner was evidenced to Peter that Gentiles received the Holy Spirit? They spoke in tongues just like all the brethren at Pentecost. The three declarations by Peter attesting to that follow:

1. "these... have received the Holy Ghost as well as *we*"; (Acts 10:47)
2. "the Holy Ghost fell upon them, as on *us* at the beginning"; (*Ibid.*, 11:15) and
3. "God gave them the like gift as He did unto *us*." (*Ibid.*, 11:17)

By Peter referring to "we" and "us" in the preceding quotes, he is including himself when declaring that the experience of Pentecost was the same as the Gentile's experience, wherein the Gentiles received the Holy Spirit and spoke in tongues. Hence Peter in fact

---

4   "The priests and rulers were greatly enraged at this wonderful manifestation, but they dared not give way to their malice, for fear of exposing themselves to the violence of the people. They had put the Nazarene to death; but here were His servants, unlettered men of Galilee, telling in all the languages then spoken, the story of His life and ministry. The priests, determined to account for the miraculous power of the disciples in some natural way, declared that they were drunken from partaking largely of the new wine prepared for the feast." (*Acts of the Apostles*, p. 40)

asserts three times that he also received the gift of tongues.

Days before Pentecost Peter hurt when Jesus questioned him, "Do you love me?" Yet moments later he wanted to know from Jesus the fate of John. (John 21:21) His aching heart did not stop his mouth even while dispirited, thus perhaps he was one of the first to begin preaching in full force to the newcomers in the tongue he had just been gifted by God's Spirit. And when the cause suffered ridicule, no wonder it was he, the one always quick to speak, who stepped forward and confronted the mockers with an arduous argumentation in favor of the truth.

Being bilingual, at times I have experienced speaking in one language with someone, but overhearing a comment in the second language I speak, find it necessary to pause in my communication to address the other person in his tongue. Something similar happened to Peter. (Acts 2:14) And since he then turned to speak to the mockers, he switched back to their language, the language of Jerusalem, presenting a defense to the accusation that he and the others were drunk, and culminating by counter-accusing them telling them they had arrested and killed Jesus by crucifying him. (vs. 23)[5]

Jesus had instructed: "Go ye therefore, and teach all nations...." (Matthew 28:16-20; Mark 16:14-18) If we research those two cites, we find that in both Jesus addressed only the eleven apostles. Does that mean that only they were to go forth, and only they received the Holy Spirit on Pentecost? No. Since dozens of

---

5 "Peter did not refer to the teachings of Christ to prove his position, because he knew that the prejudice of his hearers was so great that his words on this subject would be of no effect." (*Acts of the Apostles*, p. 41) "Some of those who listened to the apostles had taken an active part in the condemnation and death of Christ. Their voices had mingled with the rabble in calling for His crucifixion.... Now they heard the disciples declaring that it was the Son of God who had been crucified. Priests and rulers trembled. Conviction and anguish seized the people.... Peter urged home upon the convicted people the fact that they had rejected Christ because they had been deceived by priests and rulers." (*Ibid.*, p. 42-43)

tongues were represented among the visitors, only eleven apostles preaching would not have met the need of the day. Acts 2 clearly and plainly declares that all the 120 disciples received the Holy Spirit, including the women in fulfillment of prophesy. (Acts 2:16-18; Joel 2:28-29) Also, if literally only eleven persons were commissioned to do the work, well, they all died and the work is still not finished. However, by Jesus making that declaration to only the eleven apostles we are able to grasp how clearly God is a God of order. Here is why:

In the beginning spiritual sovereignty belonged to both Adam and Eve. After sin, it was reduced to males only. At the time of Abraham it was further reduced to certain males. To mark them, the circumcision was introduced. But then, during the time of Moses, that marked group was still further reduced, wherein only Levites carried on the spiritual sovereignty.

Male/Female → Males → Circumcised Males → Levites

And then came Jesus. The climax of sovereignty reached in Him, a reversal of the order, which had been established in stages, would then commence also in stages. The first step in going backwards meant expanding the ministry of the Levites by bringing into the work males from all of Israel (circumcised males). Jesus, by His authority as God's Son, did that when He appointed apostles which were not exclusive from the tribe of Levi. The next reversal step would come when all males (whether circumcised or not) would be called back into ministry. However, that work would not be done by Jesus. It was reserved for the Holy Spirit and officially commenced in the home of Cornelius, a Gentile, as we will discuss in the next chapter. Nevertheless, at that future time when the spiritual domain would increase again taking its next step in reverse, such that all males would join back into equal sovereignty with one another, there would no longer be a need for the mark of distinction among males to denote exclusivity. Hence the circumcision was bound to be done away with at its appointed time soon to come. But that time was still future, and Jesus, respecting God's established order, only ministered within the territories of Israel and only instructed His apostles, "Go ye therefore, and teach all nations..." He honored God's agenda for His time.

What a lessons there is here for us! If even the Son submits to the Father's timetable and did not usurp the work reserved for the Holy Spirit, how much more does that place a burden upon us to seek to learn God's will, way, plan, docket, method, stance, attitude *and timetable* that we may also honor all of His designations and not obstruct the work of the Holy Spirit. Rather, we are to *cooperate* with God. But we will never learn any of God's designations through words which are not even understood by the speaker of them. No. It is by digging into the Word how each individual learns the structure of Truth, while the voice of the Holy Spirit brings uneasiness or peace to the heart revealing to them God's direction at every moment.

Even among persons who are speaking the same language there may be misunderstandings. That is why we have attorneys and written contracts. Yet at times some have mentioned to me that either themselves or someone they know who does not speak English (or Spanish) has at a given time understood that language without the service of an interpreter. To satisfy my curiosity when I believe the person will not be offended, I check up on the veracity of their statement and ask, "What did you understand?" But what they tell me leaves me perplexed, sometimes more than others, because they really believe the subject was about what they claim they understood. However, even if that were to ever occur, *still it is not what happened on Pentecost*. On that day all the apostles and disciples were impacted by the outpouring of the Holy Spirit, and spoke the languages of the visitors of Jerusalem. Who understood, let's say, Peter? Those foreigners whose native tongue was the language gifted to Peter, and in which language Peter delivered his message. Who understood Matthew? Those foreigners whose native tongue was the language gifted to Matthew, and in which language Matthew delivered his message. And so it happened. The rest of the crowd understood whoever was gifted with their native tongue. Thus in this first instance regarding the gift of tongues we can see that:

1. There were various purposes for the gift of the Holy Spirit:
   a. to obey the order to preach to the world,
   b. to break the language barrier that would have impeded the work, and
   c. to eliminate in the disciples the fear of death and persecution;
2. There was a message given: We have a resurrected Savior;
3. Those who preached knew what message they had to present; and
4. The hearer of the message understood the words spoken because the disciple whom she/he listened to spoke in the native tongue of the hearer.

As a result: **The Hebrew vineyard was opened to the message of salvation.**

3

CORNELIUS, A GENTILE

Peter was given a vision in which he was ordered to eat flesh from animals which the Bible declares unclean and unfit for human consumption. (Leviticus 11) But Peter refused to eat even at a time when he "became very hungry, and would have eaten." (Acts 10:10) However, those same laws, in the minds of many Jews, including the disciples, had been applied to Gentiles, wherein the Gentiles were perceived as unclean animals who were omitted from God's salvation. By ordering Peter to eat unclean animals, God wanted to teach Peter that He favored and loved Gentiles, that salvation was also for them, and that those Peter considered unclean Peter needed to accept as his brethren.

We need to interpret the vision according to how Peter interpreted it when he exclaimed: "… God hath showed me that I should not call any man common or unclean.... Of a truth I perceive, that God is no respecter of persons: But in every nation he that feareth him, and worketh righteousness, is accepted with him." (vs. 28, 34, 35) *That* is the interpretation of the vision. Likewise, if we had slaves and receive a vision ordering us to eat unclean animals, meaning that we free the slaves, then, because we understand, we do not start eating rats and snakes but do free the slaves. In like manner, Peter correctly understood that God was spreading before him the Gentile vineyard, that he should commence in it the work of evangelization. The next reversal step in the order of spiritual sovereignty was about to take place. The circumcision, mark of distinction between males as to who belonged within the spiritual domain, no longer would be needed and was about to officially become a thing of the past.

However, although the vision triggered in Peter the conviction that Christianity is to be shared with all human beings, that conviction was still superficial in his mind and not settled in his heart as he traveled to the home of Cornelius—a Gentile who was a centurion from a company called the Italians. (vs. 1) We know this because as a precaution, knowing that his Hebrew brethren would be scandalized should they hear that he entered the home of a Gentile, Peter took six men to be witnesses of his actions. The Holy Spirit was guiding, but mankind was watching and Peter exercised prudence.[6]

Since the disciples discriminated against Gentiles, we know that those who accompanied Peter were not convinced that Gentiles are equal to Jews in God's eyes. And their prejudice became evident as the Gentiles spoke in tongues, for they "were astonished ... that on the Gentiles also was poured out the gift of the Holy Ghost." (Acts 10:45-46) If these Jewish witnesses, solely as a result of Peter's vision and prior to entering Cornelius' home, had arrived at the understanding that Jews and Gentiles are equal, then certainly they *should not* have been astonished that the Holy Spirit would descend upon Gentiles also. Furthermore, the vision alone was also not sufficient to appease the other disciples who later contended with Peter when they learned that Peter had entered the home of a Gentile. It was not until *after* Peter explained what had happened, that they rested their case and, *also astonished*, exclaimed, "Then hath God also to the Gentiles granted repentance unto life." (Acts 11:18)

Did you catch that? And who, in our own estimate, is not in

---

6 "To Peter this was a trying command, and it was with reluctance at every step that he undertook the duty laid upon him; but he dared not disobey... These were to be witnesses of all that he should say or do while visiting the Gentiles, for Peter knew that he would be called to account for so direct a violation of the Jewish teachings." (*Acts of the Apostles*, p. 137)

God's to-be-saved list? Let us read in-between the lines for who knows if someday one of us may receive a big surprise. Someone we misjudge rescues us from condemnation, because God calls all unto repentance that we may live, guiding each into spiritual growth at the rate He deems it necessary for that soul. If according to our viewpoint we regard a person as ungodly, God, Who is working with that person's heart, may surprise us by having them be the very ones who via their subsequent testimony make us witnesses of Christ-like deeds, or express to us the words of counsel necessary for our own edification. Hence the admonishment: examine everything and retain the good. (1 Thessalonians 5:21)

There are persons within our denomination that do not believe exactly as we do, and outside of it people believe many doctrines which are contrary to those we teach. Yet those stances may be independent of their ardent love for Jesus, works of mercy towards humanity, and longing to learn Truth from the Bible, which is abundant in subjects which go beyond tongues and doctrinal stand. Within all the ranks of people holding on to diversified beliefs and at different levels of spirituality, God has a people who truly loves to study and research His Word which is a fountain of knowledge.

If we eagerly research Scripture to learn about being in God's rest, or what does it mean to be humble, or whatever other theme we wish to pursue, we ought to know that God wants to guide us and give us an understanding about what we are studying as we compare verse with verse. "For precept must be upon precept, precept upon precept; line upon line, line upon line; here a little, and there a little." (Isaiah 28:10) Let us accept God's invitation, "Come now, and let us reason together," (Isaiah 1:18) and sit with God to be taught of Him, for the Bible is the only book we can read in the presence of its Author.

All Truth comes from Scripture. Therefore, it should be our

desire and goal to educate ourselves learning from It, setting out to prove our own beliefs, to correct ourselves to God's glory, as we go "To the law and to the testimony: if they speak not according to this word, it is because there is no light in them." (Isaiah 8:20) Let us allow Scripture to become our textbook for life and useful for our own teaching, rebuking, correcting and training in righteousness so that we may be thoroughly equipped for every good work. (2 Timothy 3:16-17) "Similarly, if anyone competes as an athlete, he does not receive the victor's crown unless he competes according to the rules." (2 Timothy 2:5, NIV) The rules that govern a field of learning are called disciplines. And it is God's Word that will teach us to be true disciples of Christ by guiding us to the disciplines of our discipleship. Disciples and disciplines go hand in hand.

We are all pursued by God's love and should not lightly esteem any brethren separated from our way of believing. Only God knows the heart and has a plan for each one, guiding each accordingly. In His Kingdom, all will be brought together from all walks of life, those who repent and seek to know Him that we may live, and "there will be one flock and one shepherd," (John 10:16 NKJV) for God's love in us has blossomed and bears fruit. The Father of all is calling each unto His bosom. We all need to know Scripture, and know it well.

These reflections force us to stare right into the ugly face of discrimination which results from a misconception of God. The astonishment displayed by the Jews because God gifted the Gentiles just as He had gifted the disciples on Pentecost, conclusively demonstrates what spirit reigned in the heart of the Jews, saturating them such that they believed Gentiles were the same as unclean animals. Their problem was serious, stubbornly rooted. Generation after generation helped dig it in deeper. They did not know God, even after literally beholding Him in the face of His Son. That is why the intention of the vision did not work in the

Jews the intention of God respecting the elimination of bigotry from their hearts. Hence God went a step further and gave a supernatural sign. It was quite a miracle precisely designed to eradicate quite a discrimination. When the Gentiles spoke in tongues the Jews were astonished, the vision was sealed, and their racism was radically uprooted. Jesus had said of the Gentiles, "And other sheep I have, which are not of this fold: them also I must bring, and they shall hear my voice; and there shall be one fold, and one shepherd." (John 10:16)

When Cornelius and his household spoke in tongues, could Peter and the six who came with him understand the words they spoke? Yes, indeed. They heard the Gentiles magnifying God. (Acts 10:46) Peter explained that as he and the other disciples received the gift in the beginning so the Gentiles received it. (Acts 10:47; 11:15,17) wherein in the beginning, that is, on Pentecost, those who were present *heard* in their native tongue. And so, when Cornelius and the rest of the Italians spoke in tongues, they eloquently expressed themselves in the mother tongue of Peter and the six who came with him. We must not assume that those Gentiles articulated incomprehensible syllables while the Jews wondered what they said. The record plainly states that they were magnifying God, and, if those present knew that the Gentiles were praising the Lord, it was because they were understanding them.

The impact of hearing Gentiles speak the mother tongue of the Jews was such that the racism was immediately uprooted[7] and Peter asked, "Can any man forbid water, that these should not be baptized, which have received the Holy Ghost as well as we?" (Acts 10:47) But, then, that means Peter testified to the Gentiles in a language which was not his native tongue. Well, it

---

7 "[W]ithout controversy, prejudice was broken down, the exclusiveness established by the custom of ages was abandoned, and the way was opened for the Gospel to be proclaimed to the Gentiles." (*Acts of the Apostles*, p. 142)

is logical that Peter would *not* address the Italians in Peter's own tongue, and here are two reasons why. First, even to this day we see that not all members of a migrating group learn the language of their new region. Cornelius had gathered in his home many persons comprising his family and close friends, (vs. 24) and he also had servants and soldiers, (vs. 7) for he was a centurion, that is, a Roman soldier who commanded one hundred men. In order that all may understand, it was necessary to address them in the language of said household, which was not the native language of Peter and those who came with him. And second, suppose that everyone at Cornelius' home had in fact learned the language of their new region. If that were so, when we examine Biblical maps we note that Jerusalem was about the same distance from Cornelius' home as was Judea. Acts 2 lists Judea as having a language different than the language of Jerusalem. Therefore, it is safe to conclude that also the area where Cornelius now lived had a language of its own. So, no matter what, Peter preached to the Gentiles in whatever language it was that the family unit spoke in, and which speech was not Peter's mother tongue. Peter may have already known their language before the day of Pentecost, or perhaps that was one of the languages he was gifted with on Pentecost, thus Peter was appropriately the one chosen to preach to Cornelius.

Any man could fake gibberish, but if a donkey starts a conversation, that is grounds for utter astonishment. God made a donkey speak. (Numbers 22:21-35) And if an animal can emit words intelligently because God wills it so, then we have no option but to conclude that God can do the same in humans. *And He did.* The Gentiles spoke intelligently in a new tongue: Peter's native language. Their speech was not nonsensical or gibberish. That would not have cut it with God. He means business. Gibberish would be a mockery to God's power, an insult to intelligence, and plainly *not* what happened.

In this account of the gift of tongues we learn that, again, the commission to go into all the world was accomplished.

As a result: **The Gentile vineyard was opened to the message of Salvation.**[8]

---

8   "Thus was the Gospel brought to those who had been strangers and foreigners, making them fellow citizens with the saints, and members of the household of God. The conversion of Cornelius and his household was but the first fruits of a harvest to be gathered in. From this household a wide-spread work of grace was carried on in that heathen city." (*Acts of the Apostles*, p. 139)

4

EPHESUS

The third incident mentioning the gift of tongues occurred at Ephesus, where Paul found certain disciples and asked them, "Have ye received the Holy Ghost since ye believed?" But they had not even heard about the Holy Spirit, for they had been baptized into John's baptism. Paul baptized them and laid his hands upon them, and the Holy Spirit came on them; and they spoke in tongues and prophesied. Then Paul separated them with himself and this continued for two years, so that all which dwelt in Asia Minor heard the word of the Lord Jesus, both Jews and Greeks. (Acts 19:1-10)

What is the gift of prophecy? A prophet is a person who gives God's message, but *not necessarily* because the message itself was given by God to that person. The school of the prophets of Elijah's and Elisha's day was designed not to teach how to receive instruction directly from God, but to teach God's messages to pupils who would then become prophets, that is, persons who gave God's messages. However, although receiving a message directly from God *is* within the definition of being a prophet, it *is not* the limit of its meaning. In today's world, those who are prophets more amply include persons who are preachers, evangelists, speakers, authors, teachers, mentors, etc., who give the messages found in God's Word. Thus to prophesy is the act of delivering a message, and the message is the prophecy.

The message of the disciples was salvation through a resurrected Savior. Yet these men, although disciples, had knowledge which only reached to the time of John the Baptist. But they received the gift of prophecy which meant they were able to grasp instantly, in a flash, the message Paul cherished during three years of solitude in preparation for his ministry before he started it in full force. Yet these men, via the gift of prophecy, matured instantly as proficient evangelists for Jesus. Paul, seeing what God's Spirit had done with them, separated them with himself, and together they preached in that vast area so that within the following two years, there was left not one person who had not heard, as a result of their updated discipleship, the message of salvation. But since the region of their labor was occupied by both Greeks and Jews, representing multiple languages, the gift of tongues was also given for them to skillfully do the work in the languages of the people they were to reach.[10]

Upon God imparting two gifts to these men, we see that the gift of prophecy involved giving them accurate understanding of the message Paul preached, something they would not forget after the prophecy was spoken. Similarly, the gift of tongues imparts to its recipient accurate understanding and use of the foreign language with which he has been gifted, and is not temporary but permanent. In the case of the tower of Babel, the Lord gave confusion so "that they may not understand one another's speech." (Genesis 11:7) In the case of the gift of tongues from the Holy Spirit, the Lord took

---

10 "With deep interest and grateful, wondering joy the brethren listened to Paul's words. By faith they grasped the wonderful truth of Christ's atoning sacrifice and received Him as their Redeemer. They were then baptized in the name of Jesus, and as Paul 'laid his hands upon them,' they received also the baptism of the Holy Spirit, by which they were enabled to speak the languages of other nations and to prophesy. Thus they were qualified to labor as missionaries in Ephesus and its vicinity and also to go forth to proclaim the Gospel in Asia Minor....

"For over three years Ephesus was the center of Paul's work. A flourishing church was raised up here, and from this city the Gospel spread throughout the province of Asia, among Jews and Gentiles." (*Acts of the Apostles*, pp. 283, 291)

away confusion so that men could understand each other. And when these new disciples spoke in other tongues, perhaps not all of them spoke the same foreign language, but one spoke one language, and another spoke another language, and so on. But among all of them and Paul, they spoke all the languages of that vast area where they did such an excellent work of evangelizing during the next two years. And Paul must have been very impressed with the double manifestation of the gifts of the Spirit upon these men such that he set them apart to join him in the work. Certainly Paul did not have prior knowledge, when he laid hands on them, that two spiritual gifts would be given to these new disciples. Here are two reasons why we know this.

First, the laying of hands was only a ceremonial act performed at the time specific men were initiated into an specific area of service for God, not to enable them to speak in tongues. Such is what occurred with Stephen, (Acts 6:3-6) and also with Barnabas, who is described as being full of the Holy Spirit, but it was not until at least a year later that hands were laid upon him for a specific purpose. (*Ibid.,* 11:22-26; 13:1-4) There are other more desirable attributes of the Spirit which are not gifts, but fruits. It was because of their manifested fruits that Barnabas, Stephen and others were determined by their brethren to be full of the Holy Spirit. And as a consequence of the visible fruits in their character, they were chosen to bear responsibilities within the Christian church and hands were laid upon them that the Holy Spirit might bless the particular work which they were to accomplish. While a gift is not always imparted, the fruits must exist in order to readily determine that the Holy Spirit has baptized the believer. And the fruits of the Spirit are "love, joy, peace, longsuffering, gentleness, goodness, faith, meekness, and temperance." (Galatians 5:22, 23)

Second, this experience took place in Ephesus, and when Paul wrote his letter to the Ephesians, he listed for them the gifts of the Holy Spirit, omitting the gift of tongues. Here's what Paul wrote,

"And He gave some, apostles; and some, prophets; and some, evangelists; and some, pastors and teachers." (Ephesians 4:11-12) If Paul would have placed his hands upon those men at Ephesus so that they would speak in tongues, then certainly he would have communicated the importance of that gift to the Ephesians in his letter to them. However, the fact is that he did not include the gift of tongues in the list, and we conclude that when he placed his hands upon these men, it was to initiate them officially as evangelists asking that the Holy Spirit be poured upon them for the purpose of blessing their work, not so that they would speak in tongues. However, the Holy Spirit did whatever It deemed necessary and gave the men that gift. This circumstance allows us to understand that we are not to just pray for a specific gift, but for *the gift of the Holy Spirit Itself* which has been promised to those who ask, and, additionally, we understand that the Holy Spirit further perfects our petitions as we pray.

In conclusion, if only the gift of tongues would have been imparted *without* the gift of prophecy, then we may assume that it is possible to speak in tongues and not preach salvation in Jesus, because these men only had knowledge reaching to John the Baptist. But the fact is that they were *also* invested with the gift of prophecy so that they would know what to preach—the message entrusted to the evangelist. Thus it is confirmed for us that the gift of speaking in tongues is for the purpose of evangelizing in a foreign language to people of other cultures who speak that tongue.

God honored the efforts of those men who had been carrying out His work to the extent of their understanding as disciples of John the Baptist, and advanced them to continue as evangelists, but now as disciples of Christ. In turn, since Paul had a burden to serve the Lord evangelizing other cultures, when he witnessed the two supernatural gifts bestowed upon those men, he recognized the opportunity for the Gospel in that God's grace was providing him with assistance. Thus Paul united them to himself to continue the work in Asia Minor.

Having the gift of tongues comprised the privilege of reaching other cultures, which is exactly what those men did, and thus, the commission to go into all the world remained active.

As a result: **The message of salvation continued to be preached and spread throughout both the Hebrew and the Gentile vineyards.**

5

CORINTH

Before discussing the gift of tongues in the Corinthian church, let us confirm what we have learned from the preceding three chapters as to the objective of the Holy Spirit imparting the gift of tongues:

The purpose at Pentecost: To open the Hebrew vineyard.

The purpose at Cornelius' home: To open the Gentile vineyard.

The purpose at Ephesus: To progress the work in both vineyards.

Condensing these three manifestations of tongues into one basic purpose and goal, we may establish that the gift was given to:

Enable God's people to accomplish the mission committed to them to be witnesses for Jesus from Jerusalem to the end of the earth, making disciples of all nations, and preaching the Gospel of Jesus Christ to every creature. (Acts 1:8; Matthew 28:19-20; Mark 15:15)

With this in mind, let us learn about the gift of tongues manifested in the Corinthian church by studying the letters which Paul addressed to them. Paul wrote many letters of admonition to various churches. However, we note the following about Paul's letters to the Corinthians:

1. They received two letters of admonition.
2. Both letters are among the lengthiest of the letters Paul wrote.
3. The first letter to them was Paul's lengthiest epistle.
4. In his first letter he brought to light a string of alarming issues that testified something very wrong was going on in

Corinth.

5. In Paul's first letter to them we find reproof, criticism, censure, exhortation, reprimand, and all manner of argumentation alerting the Corinthians of their ungodly condition.

The above points suggest to us the enormous importance of Paul's first epistle to the Corinthians, and as we consider the following aspects of their spirituality, we capture the urgency in Paul's message.

1. In contrast to the faith of the 120 disciples at Pentecost which were as one man, the Corinthians were divided in their beliefs. (1 Corinthians 3:3-6)
2. Among them there was so much fornication that Paul stated that not even among the heathen were performed such acts. *(Ibid., 5:1-2)*
3. They were one against the other. (*(Ibid., 6:1-10)*
4. The communion table was so perverted at Corinth that Paul stated "ye come together not for the better, but for the worse." (*Ibid., 11:17-22*)

From the last four points alone, it is clear that the Corinthians were a pitiful group. But when we read the complete letter to them, it becomes clear that they were a total mess. Yet, there is more. *They had a problem with believing the resurrection (Ibid., 15:12-24)* and that crowned their apostasy. This is quite an insight, because the resurrection is the message given at Pentecost; the message presented by Peter to the Cornelian household; and the message which was consequently prophesied by the men Paul found at Ephesus.

The resurrection is the shout of victory that makes Christianity so unique. Yet the Corinthians had a problem with it and Paul argues with them: "Because if there is no resurrection of the dead, then Christ did not resurrect. And if Christ did not resurrect, in vain then is our preaching, in vain also is your faith." (vs. 13-14)

How did Paul feel when he wrote his first epistle to the apostate church? "For out of much affliction and anguish of heart I wrote unto you with many tears." (2 Corinthians 2:4) Why was Paul filled with sorrow? Who guided the church at Corinth? Was it the Holy Spirit (with a capital "S") or was it a spirit? Who caused the Corinthians to speak in tongues? Paul lets us know by employing both words *Spirit* and *spirit*. "If you receive a *spirit* different from the *Spirit* already given to you... you manage to put up with that well enough." (*Ibid.*, 11:4) And thus we learn that the Corinthians were in fact receiving a spirit that was not the Spirit, and accepted it. Hence we rightly conclude that the spirit which controlled the Corinthians and caused them to have all the problems they had, could not have compelled them to preach salvation in a resurrected Savior because they did not even believe in the resurrection.

To analyze Paul's words to the Corinthians relating to the gift of tongues, we must consider other factors:
1. Paul suffered and cried upon writing the first letter to them. (*Ibid.*, 2:4)
2. Paul's letter was a solemn admonition (*Ibid.*, 11:4).
3. The Corinthians were carnal, divided and spiritually decaying. (1 Corinthians 3:3-6; 5:1-2; 6:5-10; 11:17-22)
4. The Corinthians did not believe in the resurrection. (2 Corinthians 15:12-22)

With this in mind, please answer this: Can you sincerely believe that the Holy Spirit was responsible for enabling the Corinthians to speak in tongues? Were they speaking other languages or were they emitting sounds without understanding what they said? The basic goal for granting the gift of tongues was to enable God's people to accomplish the mission committed to them to preach the Gospel of Jesus to the ends of the earth. Yet we repeat, the Corinthians did not go out to preach and could not have received power to go out to preach because they did not even believe in the message anyway. They did not believe in the resurrection.

What happened to the Corinth church? This is Paul's answer:

"But I fear... as the serpent deceived Eve by his craftiness, so your minds may be corrupted from the simplicity that is in Christ... And no wonder! For Satan himself transforms himself into an angel of light." (2 Corinthians 11:3, 14, NKJV)

We recognize that just as the authentic gift of tongues enabled Christ's disciples to spread Christianity, so Satan's falsification of the gift of tongues disabled the Corinthian church so that they could not make a contribution to the spread of Christianity, because they lacked belief in the very essence of the message of the disciples, the message of salvation in a *resurrected* Savior. Yet the Corinthians were indeed speaking in tongues, but as far as the verses in 1 Corinthians 14 state, and unlike what happened to the hearers on Pentecost, the congregation at Corinth did not understand the words spoken. In the following chapter we will discuss those verses in detail, which modern Christianity deceitfully interprets as follows:

1. "For he that speaketh in an unknown tongue speaketh not unto men, but unto God: for no man understandeth him; howbeit in the spirit he speaketh mysteries." (vs. 2)
   Deceitful interpretation: It does not matter if listeners fail to understand because God understands.
2. "He that speaketh in an unknown tongue edifies himself." (vs. 4)
   Deceitful interpretation: Even if a person utters sounds he himself cannot understand, he is still building himself up in the knowledge of God.
3. "For if I pray in an unknown tongue, my spirit prayeth, but my understanding is unfruitful." (vs. 14) *Deceitful interpretation:* Paul spoke without understanding himself.
4. "I thank my God, I speak with tongues more than ye all." (vs. 18)
   Deceitful interpretation: Paul was thankful because he spoke words that he himself did not understand.

5. "Forbid not to speak with tongues." (vs. 39)
   Deceitful interpretation: Do not shun tongues not understood.
6. "If I speak with the tongues of men and of angels." (Ibid. 13:1)
   Deceitful interpretation: We may be gifted with the tongues of angels even if we do not understand them.

To arrive at the authentic meaning of those verses, let us keep in mind the mental state of the Corinthians, so that we might look at those passages in the light of their understanding when Paul addressed them:

1. The Corinthians' intelligence was infantile: "Brethren, be not children in understanding: howbeit in malice be ye children, but in understanding be men." (*Ibid.* 14:20)
2. The Corinthians could not understand deep truths; thus in the past Paul had addressed them in simple, plain and clear reasoning, as one who is making an explanation to a young child. And then, while writing to them, Paul was still addressing them as if they were children: "I have fed you with milk, and not with meat: For hitherto ye were not able to bear it, neither yet now are ye able." (*Ibid.* 3:2)
3. The Corinthians' intelligence was ruled by Satan; thus they were confused: "As the serpent beguiled Eve through his subtlety, so your minds should be corrupted from the simplicity that is in Christ." (*Ibid.* 11:3)
4. A spirit was deceiving them: "If you receive a spirit different from the Spirit already given to you... you manage to put up with that well enough." (vs. 4)
5. They did not know Satan could be among them. "Satan himself is transformed into an angel of light." (vs. 14)
6. They were not accomplishing the spread of the Gospel because they did not believe in the resurrection. (1 Corinthians 15:12-22)

There is a definite difference between the term "speaking in tongues" which was given by the Holy Spirit to Paul and the rest of the disciples, and the term "speaking in tongues" which was manifested at the church at Corinth. "Speaking in tongues," when applied to Paul and the disciples, was speaking spontaneously in a *genuine* foreign language, which was previously unknown to the speaker. Furthermore, that gift was given so the recipient of it might reach people who, because of a language barrier, would otherwise never know about salvation in Christ Jesus. However, the term "speaking in tongues," when applied to the group at Corinth, suffers a change, for the Corinthians were indeed emitting sounds which were meaningless to their listeners. We then must keep in mind that Paul's letter was communicating to the Corinthians fundamental facts regarding the *authentic* gift of tongues, the gift of a real language, given for a purpose, and uttered in the presence of those who understood said tongue. Furthermore, let us remember that Paul was speaking to the Corinthians as if they were children, reasoning in simplicity, and telling them things that were fundamental facts, common sense, simple logic, which to an adult would have been unnecessary to explain. And finally, let us keep in mind that Paul suffered and cried when writing that letter because it constituted his desperate attempt to rescue them from the Satanic influence which was palpable in their midst.

6

DISSECTING THE GIFT

> *1 Corinthians 14:1-4* "*... he that speaketh in an unknown tongue speaketh not unto men, but unto God: for no man understandeth him; howbeit in the spirit he speaketh mysteries. But he that prophesieth speaketh unto men to edification, and exhortation, and comfort. He that speaketh in an unknown tongue edifieth himself; but he that prophesieth edifieth the church.*"

I am bilingual. If I were to address in Spanish a congregation that only speaks English, who would understand me? God and myself.

An older Spanish-speaking lady came to visit me and I left the living room for a moment. Upon returning, I heard my youngest son, then four years old, speaking to her in English. I told him to speak to our visitor in Spanish because she did not know English and when he had just spoken to her, the only ones who had understood were God and himself. In other words, I addressed my child reasoning such that his young mind would understand, just like in the manner Paul addressed the childish church of Corinth when he said to them that whoever speaks in an unknown tongue (a foreign language) to a person who does not understand that tongue, is merely speaking to God and edifying himself. (vs. 2, 4)

There is no halo of mystery over the term "speaking in tongues" as though it means utterance of meaningless words involuntary expressed. Biblically, speaking in tongues, when referring to the *true* gift, is plainly speaking in a real foreign language. Perhaps the reason for giving a sense of mystery to this subject arises from the fact that Paul was such a deep theologian that we actually look for a profound, complicated, abstract or supernatural explanation of 1 Corinthians 14. But the fact that Paul does not feed meat, but milk, to the Corinthians, should clarify the chapter when we study it realizing that Paul's words were simple and plain. For example, you, the reader, do not have to be told that if a German speaks in his own language to a Frenchman who only speaks French, he will not be understood. Rather, the German should speak (prophesy; deliver his message) in French. And if he does not speak French, then he should follow Paul's advice and either get an interpreter or remain silent. It is that simple.

However, since this is what Paul actually said, we must conclude that indeed the Corinthians were children in their mentality. They had to be fed only milk as nourishment for their thoughts, for their minds were ruled by Satan. No wonder Paul cried when he wrote to them! Wouldn't you also cry over having to explain trivial details such as these to an adult that you love because he does not realize that reason itself calls him to avoid speaking in German if his listener only speaks and understands French? But "rather... ye may prophecy... [because] he that prophesieth speaketh unto men to edification and exhortation and comfort." (vs. 1 and 3) That is, talk to your listeners in their own tongue so that they may be enlightened, that is, edified, by your words. Otherwise, they will be left perplexed, for all you have done is talk such that only yourself and God understood. That is what Paul meant.

***1 Corinthians 14:5** "I would that ye all spake with tongues, but rather that ye prophesied: for greater is he that prophesieth than he that speaketh with tongues, except he interpret, that the church may receive edifying."*

Why is the prophet greater than he who speaks in tongues? Since people of a common tongue remain together geographically, and preachers, unlike missionaries, reach more people within their own borders, in their own tongue, the extent of their work is greater. The purpose for prophesying (preaching) is building the church spiritually, and if it is done in a foreign language, it must be interpreted. Paul repeats this fact so many times, that there is no room for the interpretation that it does not matter if nothing said is understood.

> ***1 Corinthians 14:6-8*** *"Now, brethren, if I come unto you speaking with tongues, what shall I profit you, except I shall speak to you either by revelation, or by knowledge, or by prophesying, or by doctrine? And even things without life giving sound, whether pipe or harp, except they give a distinction in the sounds, how shall it be known what is piped or harped? For if the trumpet give an uncertain sound, who shall prepare himself to the battle?"*

Suppose the back of a church catches fire near a gas tank where there could be a possible explosion, and a passerby, seeing it, runs to alert the congregation, who still has not noticed the fire. Furthermore, suppose the passerby is a foreigner who does not speak the language of the church. How would the worshipers know their lives are in danger if they do not understand the warning? "For if the trumpet gives an uncertain sound, who shall prepare himself to the battle?" What would be the logical reaction of the worshipers? Seek an interpreter or praise God that this visitor speaks in tongues? Of course that reason itself demands that an interpreter be sought.

> ***1 Corinthians 14:14-15*** *"For if I pray in an unknown tongue, my spirit prayeth, but my understanding is unfruitful. What is it then? I will pray with the spirit and I will pray with the understanding also: I will sing with the spirit, and I will sing with the understanding also."*

Consider this statement: "For if I jump in the ocean the sharks will eat me." Does it mean that I will jump in the ocean? No. It means that I will *not* do it because then sharks would eat me. Now look again at verse 14: "For if I pray in an unknown tongue, my spirit prayeth, but my understanding is unfruitful." Does it mean Paul prayed in unknown tongues? No. It means he did *not* because, were he to do it, then he would not understand what he was saying. Notice that Paul does *not* affirm: "I pray in an unknown tongue." This verse starts with the words "for if," and we must not overlook that.

Furthermore, suppose I say to you: "For if I build a swimming pool in my back yard, next year I am going to have a party on the first day of summer. You are invited. Come with your swimming suit and towel." Then further suppose that the day for the party arrives and you have not communicated with me since the invitation. What would you do? Would you just come over ready for the swimming party, or would you call me first to find out if in fact I built the pool? If you were as excited about the party as the Corinthians were about speaking in tongues, you would probably just come over. However, since my invitation started with the words "for if," it is only logical that you call me first to find out if I, in fact, had the pool built.

In like manner, seeing that Paul's statement begins with the words "for if," we should confirm the veracity of it. Were we to do that, we would find that Paul's response follows immediately after his statement: "What is it then? I will pray with the spirit, and I will pray with the understanding also: I will sing with the spirit, and I will sing with the understanding also." (vs. 15) In other words, what some think Paul did, that is, speak in tongues without knowing what he was saying, is exactly what Paul did *not* do. Paul plainly states throughout 1 Corinthians 14 that at all times, whether he spoke, sang or prayed, he always knew what he was saying.

---

1 Corinthians 14:18. *"I thank my God, I speak with tongues more than ye all."*

Being acquainted with the original disciples, Paul probably spoke Aramaic; having been educated in the temple, he spoke Hebrew, Being a witness in Rome and a Roman citizen, he was fluent in Latin. Paul also preached to the Greeks and wrote his epistles in that language. Finally, having been chosen of God to go far and near preaching the Gospel to the Gentiles, Paul probably was fluent in many languages. How could he then not thank God that he knew how to speak many tongues, more so than the average person?

As zealous as Paul had been to destroy Christianity before his conversion, in like manner was he zealous to see it triumph when he converted. A willing missionary, eager to accomplish the will of God entrusted to him, with a heart burdened to relay to others the message of salvation, and being blessed with the ability to dominate many languages in order to quench his unquenchable desire to talk about Christ, Paul rightly exclaims: "I thank my God, I speak with tongues more than ye all."

---

1 Corinthians 14:27. *"If any man speak in an unknown tongue, let it be by two, or at the most by three, and that by course; and let one interpret."*

At any gathering, whether religious or secular, if foreigners take an active part in the discussion, they should speak by course (taking turn) while someone interprets for them. We usually see this when leaders of an organization attend meetings in areas which have been opened to their work and where a different language is spoken. However, the limit of foreigners speaking should be two, three at most, so that the trend of thought does not get interrupted excessively by having to listen first to the speaker and then to the interpreter. Otherwise the attention span of the listeners can be totally lost. However, by having only a limit of two or three persons speak in a foreign language, the audience can bear the speakers without suffering mental fatigue. Thus everyone present is benefitted and edified. And this should be done while the foreigners take turn to speak, so that the meeting is carried out in a decently and orderly fashion. (vs. 40)

By the Corinthians needing instruction in simple formalities, we discern that another spirit had affected their thinking process and was the reason for Paul stating that they still needed to be fed with milk.

---

1 Corinthians 14:29. "*Let the prophets speak two or three, and let the other judge. If any thing be revealed to another that sitteth by, let the first hold his peace. For ye may all prophesy one by one, that all may learn, and all may be comforted.*"

Even those who do speak the language of the church, when they address the congregation, should be limited to two or three persons as the rest listen. But it is understood that this should also be done while taking turn, and, if a listener wishes to add to the discussion, he should wait until he is recognized, and until the person speaking sits. These instructions for conduct and order are directed to those who speak in the language of the church and point to God as not being the author of confusion. Therefore, if the very ones who *do* speak the language of the church are to speak in turn so that no confusion results, then certainly it is expected that foreigners do the same via an interpreter. Today we raise a hand at a meeting to be recognized to speak; we learned this as children. Thus these directions again point out the fact of the Corinthians' lack of maturity and we can understand why Paul states there was another spirit among them.

1 Corinthians 14:34-35. "*Let the women keep silence....*"

Women in religion is a topic in and of itself that I would rather not deal with here. However, since Paul touches on it within the subject of tongues, these two verses are discussed in chapter 14.

1 Corinthians 14:39. "*Wherefore, brethren, covet to prophesy, and forbid not to speak with tongues.*"

To forbid not to speak with tongues simply means to allow preaching in a foreign language by a person who does not speak the language of the church, but, of course, only if her/his sermon is translated, so the listeners are edified. This happens all the time in Spanish-speaking churches in the United States when they are visited by leaders from the denominations' headquarters who only speak English. They are not prohibited from speaking, but as they preach their sermon is translated. However, what if there is no interpreter? "If there be no interpreter, let him keep silence in the church; and let him speak to himself and to God." (vs. 28) Obviously, the visiting pastor has to remain silent and pray. Mature adults do not need to be told this, and we again note why Paul felt sad for the Corinthians' mental immaturity to the point that he cried while writing to them.

> ***1 Corinthians 13:1.*** *"Though I speak with the tongues of men and of angels...."*

"Though I speak" equals to "if I speak." Paul does not affirm that he spoke the languages of angels. In 1 Corinthians 13 the subject being addressed is *love*. Love is the reason to live a life for God. If a man even suffers death for the cause of righteousness, but he does not possess God's love, his death is in vain. (vs. 3) If our words are not an expression of God's love in us, we are only making noise when we speak; and if our works express not God's love, we labor in vain.

Suppose Paul had said: "For if I fly like an angel to and fro preaching salvation, and I have not love, I am nothing." Would that mean that Paul could fly? Certainly not. By the same token, the allusion to speaking the tongues of angels is made to make us realize that love is greater, more important than the gift of speaking the tongues of angels, but not because Paul spoke the language of angels or expected to be granted the gift of speaking angelic tongues. The phrase is only a figure of speech, and it should be understood only as a figure of speech, which acts as an aid in helping us better understand the theme being discussed: the sovereignty of love.

7

CORINTH REPENTS

The simple rationalization presented in the previous chapter should bring sorrow to the sincere heart. The church Paul had instructed had gone astray. Satan was using them by making them speak unintelligently, many at the same time, and they did not realize it was a counterfeit which did not exemplify the events of Pentecost.

Paul was a profound scholar of Scripture and in his letter to the Corinthians we perceive how much he was hurting when giving such extensive explanations. The reference he made to the tongues the Corinthians were displaying was not a praise. Neither was it a lesson on how to improve what they were doing, but rather a desperate cry calling them to stop it. The debatable chapter relating to the gift of tongues should be understood as a solemn exhortation against perversion and satanic mockery.

Yet Paul's epistle did have the desirable effect in the Corinthians because, understanding from Paul's logical arguments where they had erred, they repented. (2 Corinthians 7:8-9) Nevertheless, those same words by Paul are used today by many to promote the speaking of nonsensical tongues. However, in his admonition to the Corinthians, Paul stressed the importance of being "edified." That word, in and of itself, demands an increase in knowledge and suggests expansion of already established concepts. Therefore, in the edification of a person reason and mental awareness play the main roles. If they do not and are omitted, edification is made null. To attempt to edify someone by speaking words that neither the speaker nor the listener understands, defeats the very purpose of edification for both.

Language is broken down into words which form the tools man uses to communicate information, and those words are powerful in the growth of the intellect and edification of people. The physical world of nature testifies that God intended growth to be a characteristic of his creation. Likewise, through words we grow in knowledge. But when words are not understood, growth is stunned, there is no edification, and we are left in the dark because knowledge is defeated. "My people are destroyed for lack of knowledge." (Hosea 4:6) Yet God invites us, "Come now, and let us reason together," (Isaiah 1:18) and we respond to His invitation in order to grow spiritually, but we can only be edified through words we understand.

To Timothy, Paul counsels: "Remind them of these things, charging them before the Lord not to strive about words to no profit, to the ruin of the hearers ... But shun profane and idle babblings, for they will increase to more ungodliness. And their message will spread like cancer." (2 Timothy 2:14, 16-17 NKJV)

Therefore, "speaking in tongues," as per its Biblical definition (Genesis 11:1-7) and because it is to edify, equals and means "speaking intelligently in another language words that both the speaker himself and his audience understand." Said language is concrete, sound, understandable and so very genuine that it is used by persons to communicate rationally with each other in the real world, be it secular or religious, and even their books are written in it.

Speaking nonsensical tongues predates Christianity. It was part of Pagan forms of worship even before the ministry of the Holy Spirit commenced on Pentecost. It occurs in non-Christian religions such as Santeria from Cuba, and Voodoo from Haiti, which have spread throughout the Caribbean, Brazil, Florida, Los Angeles, New York City, and other cities and countries. Those religions are a mixture of African indigenous traditions and the practice of worshiping images in Catholicism. And each Santeria spirit is associated with a Catholic image and honored during the saint's days of the Catholic calendar. Halloween's falling around that time is not a coincidence.

Those Pagan forms of religion channel to many the similar eerie influences as that of witchcraft. Their ceremonies incorporate blood sacrifices, trance, initiation, divination, and consulting with spirits. But perhaps their most captivating characteristic and phenomenon are dramatic possession rituals, which are virtually theatrical to many beholders, and their prayer methods include the use of beads reminiscent of the Catholic rosary. At such times a spirit causes one to speak spontaneously emitting unintelligible sounds that Pagan devotees claim is most like the Pentecostal and charismatic practices of speaking in tongues, which is a phenomenon that began prior to Christianity and persists to this day in both Christian and non-Christian religions, Catholicism and cults. Such senseless speech has also been associated with certain schizophrenic syndromes.

Pagan teachers advocate that the only bar to the experience of speaking in tongues is self-consciousness or fear of embarrassment, and they give a set of guidelines to attain it. Encouraging the use of "seed sounds," or any gag sound for that matter, the doorway is opened while surrendering to ecstasy, so that it ultimately commences the flow of uncontrollable, irrelevant sounds which receive the name of "tongues" and which may be accompanied by body jerks.

Thus Christians and others who desire a tongues experience may not be aware that God's Holy Spirit is guarding them against Satanic intrusion. But they sincerely believe that a display of nonsensical tongues will present an assurance of heaven's approval of themselves. Yet it is the fruits of the Spirit that should be sought; and they are "love, joy, peace, longsuffering, gentleness, goodness, faith, meekness, and temperance." (Galatians 5:22, 23) Those are the traits of character which confirm the presence of God's Spirit in the believer.

Seeking a supernatural sign would only give occasion to the deceiver to work in Christians as with Pagans. Both commence the process leading to a tongues experience in the same manner. Both are encouraged to let go and surrender self. However, by renouncing the solemn and sacred custody to their own minds, and denying themselves the God-given freedom to choose to be the rulers of their own thoughts and actions, their souls are left unguarded, which is contrary to counsel. Thus it is that the avenues to their very core are left open to be invaded by a spirit. Unintelligible sounds may ultimately be emitted. Christians, thinking that is what the disciples did to spread Christianity, believe they have been thus baptized by God's Spirit. They do not realize it is a great deception from demons. "... false prophets ... shall shew great signs and wonders; insomuch that, if it were possible, they shall deceive the very elect." (Matthew 24:24; Mark 13:22) And so it is that both Pagans and Christians alike have a similar, if not identical, tongues experience.

There are persons who claim they have been gifted with the utterance of words in a genuine foreign language. But they, unlike the experience of the disciples on Pentecost and the men at Ephesus, do not become evangelists because they themselves did not even know what they said. Thus their so called gift sabotages the very purpose for going to a region where that tongue is spoken for they did not become bilingual. That disparity never occurred with the authentic gift of tongues. As a matter of fact, they have no idea in what language they spoke in and are not the ones who claim they spoke in an authentic foreign language; rather it is someone present who tells them, and at times that other person asserts it is an ancient tongue. But how did that other person know? Was he bilingual? Was he an expert in ancient languages? If so, is there a need to evangelize anyone in that dead tongue? The more one delves into the matter, the more obvious the hoax.[11]

I asked a friend who spoke in tongues in the past, but who had abandoned the practice, "What did you use to say?" She replied, "Nothing of value." Is that how Christianity spread? Is that how the world is to hear about Christ's work of redemption, and be warned of impending plagues? Rather, it is lulling it into irresponsible sleep at a time it needs to wake up and be sober, because "the end of all things is at hand; therefore be serious and watchful in your prayers." (1 Peter 4:7 NKJV) Satan's so called gift of tongues is easily recognized as gibberish that not even the speaker of those sounds understands. Its words have no value because it is a counterfeit used to gain souls by deceit, just like counterfeit money has no value and is used to gain riches by fraud.[12]

The Bible, and parts of it, has been translated into more than 1,750 languages and dialects. Daily, tens of thousands are sold worldwide. If a foreigner moves near us and we are able to give him a Bible in his language, he will learn much more than if we speak to him thousands of words in a language that neither we, nor he, understands, and which may leave him perplexed as to our state of mind.

---

[11] "Some of these persons have exercises which they call gifts and say that the Lord has placed them in the church. They have an unmeaning gibberish which they call the unknown tongue, which is *unknown not only by man but by the Lord and all heaven.*" (*1 Testimonies for the Church*, p. 412)

[12] Such gifts are manufactured by men and women, aided by the great deceiver. Fanaticism, false excitement, false talking in tongues, and noisy exercises have been considered gifts which God has placed in the church. (*1 Testimonies for the Church*, p. 412)

"They give themselves up to wild, excitable feelings and make unintelligible sounds which they call the gift of tongues, and a certain class seem to be charmed with these strange manifestations. A strange spirit rules with this class, which would bear down and run over anyone who would reprove them. God's Spirit is not in the work and does not attend such workmen. They have another spirit." (*Ibid.,* p. 414)

Noah, in his day, gave a message. Did he give it in a language he understood? Yes. Jonah gave a message. Did he know what he was saying? Yes. Jesus, Moses, Elijah, Isaiah, Jeremiah, Ezekiel, Daniel, etc., each gave a message. Were the messages themselves given in familiar sounds? Yes. The apostles gave a message on Pentecost. Did they utter intelligible words knowing what they were saying? Yes. They spoke in languages (which were not their mother tongue) which the Holy Spirit gifted to them on that day. They knew what they were saying and their audience also understood. An edifying message was conveyed.

Had the first disciples spoken in nonsensical tongues they would not have accomplished the order committed to them to preach the Gospel. Thus it is inconceivable that in the eve of Armageddon the Holy Spirit would cause people to speak so that they themselves do not even know what they are saying. That was not the work of the Holy Spirit on Pentecost, and it will not be the work of the Holy Spirit ever. However, it was the work of evils spirits in the Corinthian church and in Pagan religions predating Christianity, and it is the work of those same spirits today. So fantastic is that work of deception that, if possible, it could deceive even the very elect. (Matthew 24:24; Mark 13:22)

Jesus foretold that signs would follow the disciples as they spread the Gospel, including speaking in new tongues (because most of the world speaks in languages different than the native tongue of the disciples), trampling on serpents and scorpions which by no means would hurt them, and drinking anything deadly that would not harm them. (Mark 16:15-18; Luke 10:17-20)

For an illustration of the sign about serpents we note an event experienced by Paul with a viper hanging from his hand. (Acts 28:1-6) But Paul did not go out of his way to handle the viper nor did he do anything for it to take place. It just happened so, and although all the people present remained watching him, awaiting for him to swell or fall down dead, no harm came to Paul.

As promised, whether Paul would have been bitten by a snake or drank poison, he would not be hurt because God had work for him to do and God was protecting him from all evil. However, that did not mean that Paul had the discretion of choosing to handle snakes on purpose or drink poison intentionally. Doing that would have been a blatant disregard for his own life by tempting God, which is a sin, (Matthew 4:7; Deuteronomy 6:16) and it would have been a presumption of, instead of faith in, His protective power. If it just so happens that we find ourselves in a death defying situation, as per His promise, God will deliver us if He deems it so. And if in any aspect we need assistance to carry out His purpose, He would gift us whatever ability we lack and open doors for us so that we successfully carry on His good pleasure. But we are not to go out of our way to intentionally put ourselves in danger like handling snakes or ingesting poison, and we are not to hunt down or stalk the gift of tongues when a foreign language vineyard is not even near us or placed within our reach.

However, in major cities, as in the United States, such multilingual vineyards do exist where thousands of foreigners have not yet learned to speak English. Nevertheless, the fact is that we may have a burden to reach those souls of different heritage, and learning some words and expressions in their language will open a door, at least socially as a start. Yet for some of them, like those from the Arab world, their religion prohibits them from reading the Bible, and they block Christianity as a way of life. But what would happen if we were gifted, suddenly, with their mother tongue? Would they listen to our message? I believe that in utter amazement they would. That would truly be the authentic gift of tongues as graced by the Holy Spirit on Pentecost, and our separated brethren would at last be reached. Wouldn't that be wonderful?

Some claim that the Corinthians were abusing the gift of tongues. But how can anyone abuse something that they do not have? It has been shown that the Corinthians' gift of tongues was a counterfeit. And so, whatever they did with it is meaningless. Thus the question is not whether those who speak tongues are doing what is proper with said gift, but rather whether they have the true gift at all.

However, let us assume that in fact some persons at Corinth who spoke a real foreign language did address the church in that tongue which was not the language of the congregation at Corinth. Then perhaps we may accommodate the description of abuse to what they were doing, although absurdity or showing off would be more appropriate. Such foolishness is backsliding, which was possible even in Peter, (Galatians 2:11) and fits the profile of those whom Paul pleaded with so that they would stop what they were doing and be ushered back into sanity. That warns us to continually walk in the faith of Jesus lest possibly, as Paul stated, "when I have preached to others, I myself should be a castaway [disqualified (NIV)]." (1 Corinthians 9:27) Likewise, we must continue to walk in the faith of Jesus in order to overcome, lest we should be disqualified and in peril of having our names blotted out of the book of life. (Revelation 3:5)

To give a live example of how it would be utterly wrong for a person to address a congregation in an authentic foreign language which they do not understand, I have presented this study bringing force to my argument by doing just that. Addressing an English speaking audience, I asserted, "What I am trying to say is..." and thereupon explained the matter quickly in Spanish, then switched back to English concluding, "and that is what Paul meant." My audience, of course, was left in limbo, but it brought home to them the reality that when I was speaking in Spanish I was only talking to myself and God. That is what Paul tried to convey. Do you copy me? Could a church be edified if that is taking place? No.

The practice of speaking to congregations in a language they do not comprehend is well over a dozen centuries old. I recall that as a child we attended the Catholic mass where Latin, a dead language, was spoken. The only part of it that lives and is taught since grade school is the Roman numerals; and that is not by coincidence given that we are called to figure out who is the beast which has a blasphemous name which number adds to 666 (Revelation 13:1, 18). Interestingly though, that verse states, "Here is wisdom. Let him that hath understanding...." (vs. 18) Everybody wants to know who is that 666, but the verse speaking of it declares that in order to know, the starting point is a mind equipped with wisdom and understanding. But for that to take place, our foundation and the take-off platform is plain and clear speech. In wisdom there is no room for blah blah blah. Yet now that Latin has practically disappeared from the assembling rituals, what has happened to the minds' understanding? Nothing much if in a given congregation that dead tongue has traded places with nonsensical tongues. The spirits of demons, like three frogs, (Revelation 16:13) are capturing their prey with their tongues within Catholicism, Protestantism and Paganism.

But it seems that there is always a remnant for God. No matter how chaotic the condition of the Corinthian church at large was, such that it warranted the lengthiest letter of admonition by Paul, with another also very lengthy letter as a follow-up, there was a small group at Corinth which did receive all of the spiritual gifts. They were a remnant, those who did not backslide. But, Who were they? "Even as the testimony of Christ was confirmed in you: So that ye come behind in no gift; waiting for the coming of our Lord Jesus Christ." (1 Corinthians 1:6-7) The remnant at Corinth stood out by the characteristic that they were waiting for the Second Coming of Jesus. In some translations it reads, "come behind in no gift those who have the blessed hope," or "waiting the manifestation of our Lord Jesus Christ." Thus in Corinth there was a small group that *did* believe in the resurrection and looked forward to Christ's return. Paul refers to those few as if by passing at the very commencement of his first letter, and then goes right into the many apostasies of the others. How do we know that there were but only a few who received all the gifts? Because Paul's letter was directed to the majority, the apostate church with many problems, including unbelief in the resurrection.

It would be prudent to assume that the remnant, unlike those who stayed behind in church speaking gibberish, went out to reach others of a different language background, just like we have seen that it was meant to be with those who received the authentic gift of tongues. Those faithful few at Corinth, which contributed to the spreading of the Gospel to the world as per our Lord's command, were not the ones Paul was bitterly crying over, and not the ones Paul desperately admonished to stop what they were doing. They were those who held fast to the "blessed hope." And today those who speak nonsensical tongues do have a problem with the blessed hope. It is known as "the rapture" or "the secret rapture."

Said Galileo Galilei, "Mathematics is the language with which God wrote the universe." And mathematics in the Bible is a heart beating, but unheard. It is the underlying common thread of Bible truths, revealing blue prints that testify of the Divine Mind of its Author, where reasoning is presented acclimatized to the field of logic, which is a branch of mathematics. In our analysis of the gift of tongues is inferred a fact which conforms to the transitive property of equality, and which formula is as follows:

If $A = B$ and $B = C$, then $A = C$.

Now, let us define A, B and C as per this subject matter.

Let A equal today's Christians who speak in tongues.

Let B equal the Corinthians at large who spoke in tongues.

Let C equal speaking in tongues by another spirit.

We know that $A = B$, because today's Christians who speak in tongues, in fact speak the same as the Corinthians at large, for they even quote 1 Corinthians 14 to back up what they do.

We also know that $B = C$, because, as we have established in this study, the Corinthians at large who spoke in tongues were speaking thus by another spirit and not the Holy Spirit.

Hence A = C. That is, today's Christians who speak in tongues which are nonsensical do so by another spirit and not the Holy Spirit.

Mathematics does not lie.

We have learned that authentically speaking in tongues as occurred on Pentecost and resulting from a gift of the Holy Spirit, is not speaking in ecstasy such that even the speaker does not understand what he is saying.

The true and authentic gift of tongues of the Holy Spirit is the gift of knowing a foreign language instantly and permanently without the human timely effort and process of learning it.

8

WORDS GOOD AND TRUE

Persons may speak that which is *good*, yet speak for Satan, and not on behalf of the Lord. Why so? It could be that their words reflect that which is contrary to what God has determined to do. An example of that is Peter's goodwill toward Jesus; yet Jesus' reply to Peter was, "Get thee behind me, Satan." (Matthew 16:23; Mark 8:33) The salvation of mankind was priority over the life of Jesus at that moment because Calvary was part of God's plan to fulfill the promise of salvation. The good wishes of Peter originated in Satan because they conflicted with God's intentions. Powerful! Some of us may have already stepped on many toes while desiring others to do what we think is good for them. It may be so, but when we ask a person, "Why don't you... ?" what we propose they do may not be God's will for them. Any of us may be guilty of this or something similar at some point. Peter surely was. We need to filter our words first through God. Good is not always best, nor right at a given point.

Persons may speak that which is *true*, yet speak for Satan, and not on behalf of the Lord. Here is an interesting passage dealing with that point. "And it came to pass, as we went to prayer, a certain damsel possessed with a spirit of divination met us, which brought her masters much gain by sooth-saying: The same followed Paul and us, and cried, saying, These men are the servants of the most high God, which shew unto us the way of salvation. And this did she many days. But Paul, being grieved, turned and said to the spirit, I command thee in the name of Jesus Christ to come out of her. And he came out the same hour." (Acts 16:16-18)

Wow! This damsel pointed to Paul as a servant of the most high God who taught the way of salvation, yet she did it while demon possessed. Why? First, she overpraised Paul, and second, her repetitions disrupted God's work interfering with that which should have been carried out decently and in order. (1 Corinthians 14:40) What an eye opener!

I recall a day when a utilities worker came to fix a minor problem in my home. During his short stay, as he explained the cause of the problem, with every few words he spoke he interrupted himself by wishing me, "May Jehovah bless you." After he had repeated that over ten times within ten minutes, I wondered if I should declare, "I command thee in the name of Jesus," but did not. Remember, Paul was patient for many days. But how long would Paul tolerate such behavior in a church? Is there such a thing as overdoing it? The way Paul handled the situation shows us that there is.

Sometimes emotions are summoned through repetition via a new genre of songs which have been labeled "seven-eleven music." A mantra of some seven words is chanted to the same tune about eleven times in succession. However, repetition, even in prayer, is against divine counsel. "But when ye pray, use not vain repetitions, as the heathen do: for they think that they shall be heard for their much speaking." (Matthew 6:7) Hence even speaking repeatedly the same praise over and over and over and over, may become a hypnotic tool, is disruptive, and shifts the praise from God to the preacher, which may not be what that soul (the preacher) needs. Peter did not allow men to bow down before him. (Acts 10:25-26) John fell down to worship before the feet of the angel who presented to him the apocalyptic visions, but the angel told him not to do it and to worship only God. (Revelation 22:8-9) Though we may not be literally kneeling to worship a man, the build-up of vocalized praises serves the same purpose; and, further, in overpraising passion-like feelings take over and reason goes out the window. But feelings are not faith.

Truth is eternal. Excitement wears off. Hence excitement is not Truth. Therefore, what spirit is it that causes persons to continually and loudly utter praises and allow themselves to enter an accelerated and thrilling emotional condition, even if it disturbs the speaker's trend of thought, and even if it lacks consideration for others who need to listen without distraction? Whatever happened to Paul's counsel, "if anything be revealed to another that sitteth by, let the first hold his peace [keep silent, NKJV]"? (1 Corinthians 14:30) Yet, in such cases of disruption through repeated praises such persons have nothing edifying to add.

"But the Lord is in his holy temple: let all the earth keep silence before him." (Habakkuk 2:20) When a person is presiding and edifying the body of believers, silence should reign that all may hear the Word, for "faith comes by hearing." (Romans 10:17) If Paul were officiating, since he did not put up with the damsel who upheld his work, certainly Paul would not tolerate voiced emotions for long and would rebuke the evil spirits. Outside of the church setting, such repeated, continuous interruptions may also cause rebuke, but in other ways. At a theater, they may cause a person to be escorted out. During trial, they may cause a person to be held in contempt of court. At a company meeting the employee's behavior will not go on unchecked. And in a classroom setting it will not be permitted. But in church, it is mothers with small children who are likely to be set apart, and not disrupting adults.

The lessons presented by the damsel incident and the verbalized interruptions characteristic at Corinth (1 Corinthians 14) show that continuous praise and affirmation caters to human passion rather than the intellect and is totally unacceptable. "Wherefore gird up the loins of your mind, be sober ... be holy in all manner of conversation ... pass the time of your sojourning here in fear." (1 Peter 1:13, 15, 17) Anyone of us may at some point spontaneously emit a sound of wonderment due to our intellect being impacted by truth presented. But the danger lies when those verbalizations go on unchecked and are nurtured into habit, so that ultimately our spirit shifts into the emotional gear by being built up through vain repetitions. As clearly as Abel understood what offering to bring that would be pleasing to the Lord, we should also understand what behavior we should bring before the God of the universe.

And why are we applauding our preachers? Entertainers are applauded, but not preachers. If I pass the pastor in the hallway or in the parking lot, and he stops for a one-to-one chat with me, and tells me the same thing he would preach from the pulpit, should I applaud him? No. We don't applaud people who converse with us. So why should we do it if the same message is delivered in a sermon? I believe it may be because we have been dedicating so much time to the overwhelming amount of entertainment the world has to offer, that we have lost the capacity to distinguish between what is holy and what is mundane. So we applaud our preachers, though a hearty "Amen" at the conclusion of a sermon would suffice.

Unconsciously, we are beginning to view our preachers as entertainers, and many of them have started to behave as such. They foment drama and instigate endless praises by bringing in a lot of clutter to the delivery of their message, like abrupt body jerks, theatrical facial expressions, gesture freezing, nonsensical tongues, the old chanting updated to a jazzy tune, or even repeating a key phrase that they hammer in for long periods, together with all manner of entertainment techniques that help turn worshipers into emotion-fed spectators. Is exhilaration the trendy way to go when a body of believers gets together? Whatever happened to "Be still, and know that I am God"? (Psalms 46:10) Many move to and fro like caged, wild animals, or showing no honor and respect for God's written Word, they bang and flap the Bible keeping everyone in awe of their audacity. Must one get into a bad mood, or have an attitude of defiance, in order to speak about Truth? Amazingly, the more rage that is displayed, the more in-your-face and with imposition the message is barked out, the better some congregations seem to like it, although something similar is what occurs in rock concerts. And all the while, with whatever method is used at the gathering, accompanying emphasis music in the foreground is non-stop to maintain a hold on the emotions. When all is said and done, the mind remembers the extravaganza and triggers the heart to feel again the passion, provoking it to thirst for more thrill.

In contrast, Jesus many times preferred speaking from a fishing boat as the breeze carried His voice to the crowds sitting and listening on the shore. Had Jesus, while speaking to them, acted out agitated, certainly He would have literally made waves and the boat would have been in danger of capsizing. But Jesus is He Who calms the sea, (Matthew 8:26-27; Mark 4:39-41) not One to cause the waters to swell. And since waters also represent people, (Revelation 17:15) hence Jesus, just as He calmed the sea, must have also appeased the spirit of His listeners by His attitude, His demeanor, and His behavior as He taught them, while soothing them with words of hope and consolation. Such is our example. Listening thus to Jesus, when all is said and done, the mind reflects upon His teaching and thus commences the renewing of our minds, while God's Word in our hearts, like a fountain of living waters, quenches our desires for Him with Heaven's peace and contentment.

Because of the Lord's example, it would be appropriate for us to cultivate our speech giving God our best in that too. It requires effort and training, sacred duty we owe to our children, the church and our message. A respectable documentary is a good example of how professionals transmit their message. But ours is *The* Message. Accordingly, let us polish our speech. "Be holy in all manner of conversation." (1 Peter 1:15) The church family should take an active part in speaking gracefully, otherwise we help stagnate others, especially children and adolescents, in how they speak and thus perpetuate their disadvantage. But, amazingly, many churches lien more and more on a display of nonsensical tongues. Yet what could be more fruitful to our message, elevating to our character, and a service to the church at large and our youth in particular, striving to improve our everyday speech, or going after a nonsensical tongues experience?

Consequently, bilingual parents need to teach their children both tongues they speak because, should they grow up and choose to work for the Lord, the more languages they command, the more people they can reach with the message of salvation. Such training calls for families to strive to speak among themselves, in particular if there are young children, only in their language of origin. That is how the structure of that language—which we acquire subconsciously by instinct and later on in life learn is called its grammatical rules—becomes firmly anchored, to later be polished through literature and interactive communication, perhaps even travel, as a grand preparation that God may use at the appropriate time. Those who are not given this advantage, starting from their birth and persevering continually, usually end up never learning well the language of their ancestors. That is because peers are many while parents are two at the most. Hence there is more of an opportunity to speak the language of the region, and if the atmosphere of the home absorbs that tongue, chances are the family heritage will become a thing of past generations and the children will not be competent bilingual persons. But if the goal is preparation for working in the spread of the Gospel should they be called of God, learning to discipline ourselves such by getting them ready is well worth the effort.

But most important of all, however, is that our words reflect God's will. Above we examined speech conveying a message which was *good* because the motive was goodwill, and speech which was *true* because it praised God's work. But, regardless, we beheld a controversy when we considered how Jesus and Paul each respectively handled the situation. It turned out that both messages were entirely contrary to God's plan and blocked His will. And if even Peter became a victim of evil spirits through good words, what about us? That means we have a grand responsibility regarding evaluating the words of a language we understand. Hence greater still should be our interest in teaching our church family to question why some speak without an idea of what in the world they are saying.

9

INTERPRETATION

The gift of interpretation is considered to be the ability to translate nonsensical tongues. Yet, authentic interpretation is being able to translate from one language into another by someone who knows both languages well and who can communicate intelligently in both languages at *all times*. Hence an interpreter is a person who is bilingual and has a unique gift, for not all bilingual persons can interpret or translate, just like not all who play a musical instrument can play it by ear. Professionally, the word "interpret" is used when referring to oral communication, while "translation" is applied to written communication. I will use them interchangeably here.

Some interpreters err in that they do not communicate many expressions correctly, or do so transmitting a weaker or different impact than that of the original language. Those who do that are bilingual persons who either do not have the gift of interpretation or were not well versed in the subject at hand. Some interpreters at times render the negation of the statement made because they either were not paying full attention or did not understand the words correctly. Sometimes speakers do not pause to give an opportunity to the interpreter to translate in small sections at a time, and their statement become too long to remember in its entirety, thus an accurate and complete translation cannot be rendered.

An interesting variation of that gift is the ability for simultaneous interpreting, meaning that at the same time that an orator speaks in a foreign tongue, the interpreter renders the message in the language of the audience. Such persons may be employed, for example, at international events. It truly requires a gift plus full concentration, a sound knowledge of the subject matter, and mastery of both languages in order to interpret instantly, correctly, and accurately.

At an evangelistic series in my church when I acted as a simultaneous interpreter, I had to keep up with the pastor's pace as the words entered in English into my ears via the headphones I was wearing, and came out in Spanish from my mouth. And when he said something personal, for example, "my wife" I did not render "he says that his wife." No. I also said in Spanish, "my wife," because I was only his mouthpiece. At the conference I sat apart in a room at the rear joined by those who did not speak English, and we viewed the speaker in the sanctuary through a large glass section of the wall. That way my delivery of the sermon in Spanish would not cause any distraction. And it served for the spiritual edification of all, as meetings are to be carried out decently and orderly as prescribed by God. (1 Corinthians 14:40) Fortunately, the preacher did not use an acrostic (a list of words which initials form another word usually vertically). Such creative highlights within a presentation cause interpreters to pause figuring out how to best translate so that the message makes sense. If the pause is too long, they may have to skip that part altogether, and the edification of the audience will be affected at that point, but not like in nonsensical tongues. In authentic interpreting, the interpreter may discuss later with the speaker how to translate the message in order to improve upon its rendition the next time that acrostic is used. But in the interpretation of nonsensical tongues, the so called interpreter cannot check up with the speaker of tongues because the speaker himself did not even know what in the world he was saying.

The necessity for good interpreters is required when many languages are represented in a given region, such as the territories to where the Gospel spread. Knowing that the areas where

Christianity first commenced had the particular characteristic of multiple languages, the need for precise interpreting was utterly essential. Hence God's Spirit deemed bestowing this gift so that the work may not suffer. If there was no one to speak in tongues, in the language of the listeners, then a good interpreter would supply the deficit.

Projects like the translation of a book require good translators. Yet, comparing two translations of the same work by each of two interpreters who are genuinely bilingual persons with the gift for interpreting, renders that each translates basically saying the same thing. If a mural is illuminated with alternating blue and red lights, variations are seen in it as the projection of the different rays are cast upon it. Shades change, the mood changes, but the mural is still the same. The observer of it when the light was red can speak to the person who saw it when the rays were blue, and both understand that it portrayed a medieval battle, if that is what it was. However, if one sees the mural as a carnival in Rio and another as a boat show at the marina, be assured that both viewers were hallucinating. That fallacy in translation has not happened to the Bible.

God has protected His Sabbath in spite of traditions. He has protected His people amid centuries of persecution. And, likewise, he has protected His Word through Its many translations. Yet the Bible has been the target of rejection with the excuse that translations may not be a valid rendition of the original writing. Why not use the same argument to shun the writings of philosophers of long ago? Because the Bible is Satan's prey. But in my beholding that both English and Spanish translations of the Bible sketch the same design and emit the same hues, then, since *the Spanish and English Bibles each came via a different line of translations*—they are not direct translations of each other—it proves to me that I am in fact studying the authentic Word of God which God protected from assault and distortion. Savoring that assurance is one of the numerous advantages of being bilingual. Yet, as pertains to the interpreters of nonsensical tongues, there is no original to compare it to because the author of nonsensical tongues did not himself have an idea of what he said. Probably not even God and his angels know what was said because nonsense does not convey anything.[13]

In reference to some persons who claim to be able to interpret nonsensical tongues, we note that, for starters, such persons are usually not bilingual in the real world; but further, they definitely do not speak the so called tongues they assert they can interpret. It is all in their imagination or planted in their minds by a spirit as part of the display of that which borders on the fantastic to convey the presence of a supernatural power which is not from the Lord. The practice is even absurd. Suppose at a meeting we all speak English and one person starts uttering nonsensical tongues to give a message. Another person interprets it so that we all know what was said. Hello? Wouldn't it be easier for the first person to just say it in English?

Some have claimed that, over and over, these persons who claim they have the gift of interpretation render each a totally different translation of the same utterance; and that sometimes foreigners admit that a few of the nonsensical tongues words were in their mother tongue, but the words were profanity and/or curses to God. Though I have heard about that, I cannot attest to its veracity. One thing I know is that I told a lady who started babbling her tongues, to stop and talk in Spanish or English. Immediately she shut up and seemed confused. But I do not have the power, nor the authority, to shut up the Holy Spirit. Do you grasp what I am saying?

In order to render an interpretation as correct as possible, some attorneys hire female interpreters for female clients, and male interpreters for male clients. Some believe that even the demeanor of the interpreter should match the demeanor of the person for whom they are translating, especially for declarations by witnesses in court before a jury. If this is what the world does, why should the church condone a practice that is totally illogical and unnecessary,

---

13 "... *unknown not only by man but by the Lord and all heaven.*" (*1 Testimonies for the Church*, p. 412)

i.e., nonsensical tongues and its so called interpretation? Because it is following an agenda not of the Lord.

In general, people are unfamiliar with legal terminology. The average person cannot soundly explain in detail what a legal document states, and I am speaking about explaining in your own language a document which is also written in your own language. Even in simple conversations two persons who are speaking the same language many times misunderstand each other. Do we truly need more disorientation? Unintelligible tongues coupled with interpreters who are not bilingual? Are we becoming a house of confusion?

A word of advice before closing this chapter: If you are a preacher needing a simultaneous interpreter, please do not assume that because a person is bilingual that they can interpret. There are rules of thumb to adhere to. First, observe if the person is literate and speaks English clearly and gracefully. Those attributes are expressions of character that remain in both languages. Second, do not choose persons who come across as literate but who are hard to understand. Their problem may be more than just a heavy accent. On two occasions I could not understand a Hispanic who spoke English as if they had a spoon in their mouth, so I switched to Spanish assuming that I would then understand them. But the spoon remained because that is the way they talked, sort of like having a speech impediment. Therefore, make sure their accent is really just that. Third, if it is a local meeting, choose persons who are literate and well versed *in Spanish* (*cum laude* please) way past high school, but if the presentation will be delivered via satellite or the media unto other areas and countries, please employ a God-fearing, professional interpreter, a believer knowledgeable in the subject matter you will be sharing, and meet with them first. And fourth, choose persons whose demeanor would represent you best.

Persons who have the gift of interpretation have dominion of *both* languages used in their translation.

10

MIRACLES

The Lord God spoke, and it came to pass. Instantly. Likewise, when Jesus commanded, miracles occurred as soon as He spoke. Miracles involve creation. Blind men receive sight, the lame walk, lepers are cleansed, the dead are raised, the deaf hear, the dumb speak, the maimed are made whole, and many are cured of infirmities and plagues, and evil spirits. (Matthew 11:5, 15:31; Luke 7:21-22) All miracles Jesus performed match the power of the Word of Creation. The disciples, in the name of Jesus, also performed miracles which happened immediately. (Luke 10:17; Acts 3:6-7)

However, the devil is not a creator and resorts to miracles of a lower nature. For example, in the medical field, a patient who needs a tumor removed is first anesthetized. The surgeon operates on him and then the patient regains consciousness. Such is the miracle of modern medicine. And such remarkable technique was developed by Satan himself, for the people fall unconscious seeking a miracle. When they come to, some claim they are cured. Where in the Bible is that process of receiving a miracle found? Nowhere. Did Jesus perform miracles requiring people to fall unconscious first? No.

Jesus came to raise people, raise the dead, raise the sick from out of their bed. Jesus lifts up. He does not bring down. I am compelled to repeat this. Jesus came to raise people, raise the dead, raise the sick up from their bed. Jesus lifts up. Satan is the one that throws people to the ground. (Mark 9:18; Luke 4:33)

The term for such happening is called "slain in the spirit," and it is also claimed that such it is that folk receive the Holy Spirit. However, in Scripture, when Jesus breathed upon His disciples saying unto them, "Receive the Holy Spirit," He then continued speaking to them. (John 20:22) But if in fact people fall unconscious when they receive the Spirit of God, then, if the disciples had fallen unconscious, who did Jesus continue talking to? Himself? That is absurd. Nothing in Scripture validates being slain in the spirit. Paul, on his way to Damascus, did not become unconscious when Jesus appeared to him, but what did happen is that the glorious light blinded him for three days. But Paul distinctly remembered the event and the dialog he had with Jesus. Also the men who accompanied him heard the voice of the Lord. (Acts 9:1-9) Furthermore, when the Holy Spirit came upon the 120 praying disciples on Pentecost, they were not stricken unconscious to the ground. Rather, from their praying posture they rose to their feet and went out the door to begin the spread of Christianity in full force, and they were very much awake, aware and alert. The religious practice of losing consciousness for a period of time without later recalling what occurred during that time has its roots in the occult's trance stages. It also takes place if we give up control of our mind to be hypnotized.

Supposedly, when a preacher who claims to perform miracles in the name of Christ touches a person, most often on the forehead, and that person falls back slain in the spirit, one of the preacher's assistants catches the person as they drop and then leaves them laying on their back on the floor. Flipping through the channels I happened to come across such a telecast. Music captured the souls setting the desirable atmosphere, and the collapses began. However, I noticed one man was careful enough to turn himself around first so that he would lay on this stomach, and then turned his head not to have his face against the floor; and a woman, right after the assistant left her, fixed her blouse and then continued laying there. Were they acting? Some had spasms which do occur in possession rituals. Others gave testimony of having been healed days earlier and then the preacher touched them and down each went. Weren't they already healed? Those who, after having laid on the floor, got up, fell back to the floor because the preacher again touched them, and sometimes from afar by merely blowing towards them they fell; and he beamed acknowledging a power present exercising his will. The crowd, thrilled, applauded a proceeding which the Bible does not support.

During a documentary which promoted miracles, I had to leave the room for a moment while a renown preacher was being interviewed. It was not until I was only listening and not viewing him that it dawned on me that there was something different about his voice, so different that I thought it was someone else and for a moment went back to confirm it was him. I left the room again and listened in wonderment at his almost perfect tone such that he did not sound like his usual self. But there was something else still which I could not pinpoint, and then it hit me. His trademark accent was gone. Amazed, I went back to view him. Concentrating on his mannerism, I realized that every time he made a statement that specifically served to affirm his ministry of miracles, he fluttered his eyes. Again and again he only blinked rapidly when he vocalized the veracity of the healings. He did not do it at other times, and he did it every time he bore witness to the miracles.

The next day I began researching body language studies, and read articles on various websites dealing with detecting deception. Relating to voice change, "When someone you know makes a statement with emphasis using a different voice tone to normal. Pay attention! When someone lies there is often an effort to try too hard to be convincing and this will show up in their voice." And from the FBI's website here is a cite about eye movement, "[I]ndividuals who struggle with an idea or concept often blink their eyes rapidly. Rapid blinking or 'eyelid flutter' signals a sensitive topic. Officers carefully should observe the speaker's eyes, which can alert to the possibility of deception."

Further I happened to come across a web page containing that evangelist's testimony and his experiences in necromancy (talking to the dead). Obviously such practice is prohibited by God, (Deuteronomy 18:10-11; Isaiah 8:19-20) and makes his ministry, in my observation, full blown spiritualism.

On another televised event, a visiting preacher from South America with the stroke of his arm that he threw up gesturing, caused a group of local pastors to fall back unto the floor that they would receive the "holy spirit." My friend's mother, an elderly woman also watching the phenomenon, in amazement asked, "Did they not already have the Holy Spirit?" What an excellent observation! What spirit did they have before the visiting pastor came along? If they are pastors it is logical for one to assume they are being guided by God's Spirit. At least one hopes so. But the reality is that the happening has no Biblical backup that would render it to be a necessary spiritual experience from God, and further, we should not be testing the Holy Spirit. Testing the Spirit of the Lord is what Ananias and Sapphira did, and they did fall down, but dead. (Acts 5:1-10) So a "slain in the spirit" event is produced by Satan who brings down people. (Luke 4:33; Mark 9:18) But not Jesus; Jesus raises people.

This fact, then, made those pastors leaders who are themselves without a knowledge of Scripture, for had they been acquainted with God's Word they would have known the practice of slaying in the spirit is not Biblical. "Do ye not err, because ye know not the scriptures...?" (Mark 12:24) Hence, those who pretended to be the mentors of God's sheep did themselves surrender to forces and guidance outside of the Holy Writ.[14] That awareness makes it the more evident to each of us that we are on our own alone with God, which, consequently, is the way it should be.

How did Jesus conduct Himself? He reached out tenderly pleading with men's hearts. Speaking from a fishing boat, the people were separated from Him and were beyond the reach of His healing touch. But people gathered regardless because there was more to Jesus than just miracles. They came to hear Him, feeding their spirit with Him, the Living Word. They did not come for the drama to indulge themselves with passions provoked by a "slain in the spirit" spectacle that certainly would have sent men overboard. So also we should seek the nourishment of God's Word over and above outward manifestations which the world embraces, and many times demands, as proof that God has anointed.

Some explain that miracles are happening everywhere, such as a person who had a glass eye and now sees through it. Satan cannot create living cells, hence a real eye, like Jesus would do. I have been told that toothaches disappear as dental cavities are supernaturally filled. Satan cannot create a living nerve or bone tissue, hence a brand new human tooth with the very same DNA of the individual, but Jesus can do it. I was also told a man with a deformed face went to sleep firmly believing a miracle would happen to him, and when he woke up the next morning his face

---

14 "Eve really believed the words of Satan, but her belief did not save her from the penalty of sin. She disbelieved the words of God, and this was what led to her fall. In the judgment men will not be condemned because they conscientiously believed a lie, but because they did not believe the truth, because they neglected the opportunity of learning what is truth. Notwithstanding the sophistry of Satan to the contrary, it is always disastrous to disobey God. We must set our hearts to know what is truth. All the lessons which God has caused to be placed on record in His word are for our warning and instruction. They are given to save us from deception. Their neglect will result in ruin to ourselves. Whatever contradicts God's word, we may be sure proceeds from Satan." (*Patriarchs and Prophets*, p. 55)

was restored. Doctors also perform plastic surgery when people are unconscious.

So many signs and wonders are around us that we cannot afford to forget the clear warnings about Satanic manifestations:

- "Will surely deceive, if possible, even the very elect." (Matthew 24:24)
- "And he doeth great wonders, so that he maketh fire come down from heaven on the earth in the sight of men, And deceiveth them that dwell on the earth by the means of those miracles which he had power to do." (Revelation 13:13-14)
- "Even him, whose coming is after the working of Satan with all power and signs and lying wonders." (2 Thessalonians 2:9)

Furthermore, we are encouraged to *not* believe in manifestations, but are to investigate whether or not they are from God, and we should know the Spirit of God. "Beloved, believe not every spirit, but try the spirits whether they are of God; because many false prophets are gone out into the world. Hereby know ye the Spirit of God." (1 John 4:1-2) We are not to attribute all we see to the Holy Spirit and must question those signs and wonders. "If there arise among you a prophet, or a dreamer of dreams, and giveth thee a sign or a wonder, And the sign or the wonder come to pass, whereof he spake unto thee, saying, Let us go after other gods, which thou hast not known, and let us serve them; Thou shalt not hearken unto the words of that prophet, or that dreamer of dreams: for the Lord your God proveth you, to know whether ye love the Lord your God with all your heart and with all your soul." (Deuteronomy 13:1-3)

God "proveth" us, tests us, and it is in the language of beliefs and works that we give testimony of whom we serve. When those who claim to perform miracles present doctrines and beliefs, of course they are not going to openly declare, "Let us go after other gods." However, if their guidance is not consistent with Scripture, they are basically calling us to follow other gods. Doctrines may or may not defy God's authority, and the same are affirmed by the power behind the miracles, God or Satan. But God will not affirm with a miracle, a practice that contradicts His Word. And so, since it is a fact that many miracles call us to follow certain beliefs and rituals, among which are the nonsensical tongues and the fainting process denoted "slain in the spirit," we can be sure that the miracles are not from God. If they were, then God would be contradicting Himself causing His people to glorify Satan, while at the same time we know God wants to save his people from the snares of the devil, and is calling them out of confusion. (Revelation 18:4) This contradiction with respect to God is then another proof that the miracles are not originated in Him, and those miracles are nothing more than spiritualism at its best.

Moreover, it is not up to us to demand a miracle and expect it to happen. God may not will to heal a person. Timothy was ill and there was no healing for him, rather, Paul suggested a course of action to follow so that Timothy may deal with his own health problems. (1 Timothy 5:23) And as to Paul, God *did* restore his sight, (Acts 9:17-18) but *did not* take away a painful physical ailment even though Paul wanted to be fully restored and pleaded with God about it three times. (2 Corinthians 12:7-10) Likewise, we are to pray for healing, but whether we will receive the miracle, we do not know, as Paul and Timothy did not receive certain miracles.

God's cure goes beyond the physical. He wants to heal us spiritually. When Paul's sight was restored, God simultaneously and additionally healed him spiritually by giving him the Holy Spirit. (Acts 9:17) We have God's sure promise that He will give His Spirit to those who ask, (Luke 11:13) thus spiritual healing is guaranteed. God *may or may not will* to physically heal us, but He *does will* spiritual healing for those who ask for the Holy Spirit.

The reason why we may not receive physical healing may be because God deems that we will grow spiritually through a physical malady. Paul declares, "... to keep me from exalting myself, there was given me a thorn in the flesh ... I entreated the Lord three times that it might depart from me ... He has said ... 'My grace is sufficient for you, for my power is perfected in weakness.'" (2 Corinthians 12:7-10) To safeguard Paul's spirituality, God allowed his malady to remain. And to safeguard our heart, God may at times allow infirmities and hardships if He deems that they serve as tools to do just that. "For we know that all things work together for good to them that love God." (Romans 8:28) Paul wrote, while a prisoner in a dark, humid dungeon, "Rejoice in the Lord always. And again I say, Rejoice." (Philippians 4:4)

Jesus heals us spiritually: He "brought Good News to the poor, proclaimed liberty to the captives, restored sight to the blind, set free the oppressed, and preached the acceptable year of the Lord." (Luke 4:18-19) How was it possible? He said, "The Spirit of the Lord is upon me." (*Ibid*. 4:18) If we allow the Spirit of God to mold us, our spirit, meaning our very core and character, even our own righteousness, becomes impoverished and what stands out is the righteousness of Jesus in us. And it should not matter that the righteousness of our spirit decreases, for "We are all as an unclean thing, and all our righteousness are as filthy rags." (Isaiah 64:6)

In His Sermon on the Mount Jesus opened with what is known as the Beatitudes, which very first declaration is, "Blessed are the poor in spirit, for theirs is the kingdom of heaven." (Matthew 5:3) Less of our spirit, our own ways, and more of His Spirit, His will, depletes our spirit and is what makes room for God's Spirit, that we be steered into God's kingdom, *if we follow Jesus.*

11

PROVE THOSE IN MINISTRY

Beware of whom ye follow. In the work of surrendering, it is Jesus Whom we must follow. Therefore, we must beware, lest we mistakenly are lead to trail after another man's spirit, surrender to his will, and ultimately participate in the assassination of our own spiritual perception of truth. In the past few decades, some have even taken the next bizarre step: suicide. Amazingly, it is not one person at random who is involved in such an incomprehensible act for religious reasons, but entire congregations, sometimes numbering in the hundreds, have ended their lives by participating in horrific mass suicidal ceremonies as per the instructions of a shepherd of death whom they were deceived into following.

We must be alert at all times because the act of surrendering our spirit in exchange of another is not a guarantee that the Holy Spirit will be the one that will abide in us. No. We are to make sure that we never attach ourselves to a branch that we think is attached to Jesus or looks like it is attached to Him. We ourselves have the privilege, as sons and daughters of God, of being attached *directly* to the True Vine. So we are not to live in the shadow of another's views, ways and rituals, and are not to take people to them. We may invite folk to our church because we have a great pastor whom we love and respect. There is nothing wrong with that *if* he/she leads them to Jesus, Who is still beyond our pastor and Who is the focus and goal for each of us.

Be ye therefore Christ's follower without a human intercessor or agent. Pastors and priests are not good enough because they also need Christ. Some of them have been in the news under a negative light. Moreover, history reveals that some the worse crimes have been committed in the name of religion. The leaders of Judaism were successful in their request to the Romans to have Jesus crucified, and they then persecuted their own kin, the early disciples. Catholicism is tainted with the blood of millions of Christians who, during the middle ages, were forced to live in caves and catacombs, and when captured were tortured and killed throughout Europe as a result of its Crusades and barbaric Inquisition. That agency in Spain worked to confiscate Bibles that the Protestant movement was making available to the people, and sentenced the Christians to be burnt alive sealing their faith as martyrs. (See *The Missing Chapter from The Great Controversy*[16]) But amazingly, when Protestantism secured political power it too turned to persecution resulting in the exodus of the Pilgrims and first settlers seeking a new land where they could worship God in peace. Then, in the New World, many Protestants promoted slavery and illiteracy for slaves. That meant that ultimately some of those who upheld the reading of Scripture were keeping a people ignorant of the necessary skill to do just that! And religions outside of Christianity are no better. Presently, in the United States, were it not for its Constitution which separates church and state, we would not have the freedom to worship which we now enjoy. Let us then use our liberty to diligently study Scripture for ourselves that we may see spiritually.

We need the sight of our spiritual eyes restored. Jesus "brought Good News to the poor, proclaimed liberty to the captives, *restored sight to the blind*, set free the oppressed, and preached the acceptable year of the Lord." (Luke 4:18-19) Notice the miracle

---

16 *El Despertar de España (The Awakening of Spain)* was included —with permission from Ellen G. White — as Chapter 13 in *The Great Controversy* published in Spanish. That extra chapter by itself as a book is available in English via TEACH Services and titled: *The Missing Chapter from The Great Controversy*

of sight, although in other Bible verses is included within the list of miracles which were physical and which Jesus performed, in this particular verse it is listed among events that bring rays of truth to the mind. Jesus opened the spiritual eyes of His listeners as they received His words when He taught them. To see spiritually is to understand. (Ephesians 1:18) In one instant, it is said that the literal blindness of one man was allowed "that the works of God might be displayed," (John 9:3) for God's intension was also that the manner in which He healed that man's physical condition would serve as a spiritual lesson for those of us who need to see spiritually. We need to be rescued from damnation by receiving the miracle of spiritual eyes that see.

Scripture further invites and encourages us to prove those in ministry. "Thou hast tried them which say they are apostles, and are not, and hast found them liars." (Revelation 2:2) When Paul was scrutinized by a group of believers, his reaction was to compliment them for questioning even him, and declared them to be nobler than those who did not question what they were taught. (Acts 17:10-11) Further Paul states that if he himself should contradicts God's Word, he should be accursed (eternally condemned); and if even an angel contradict's God's Word, that angel should likewise be accursed. (Galatians 1:8-10) Those are powerful words that ought to wake us up. So let us follow through with the advice given to us and test those in ministry, for it is our eternal life that is at risk. We are the interested party in this concern, and that makes it our responsibility to seek the way of our own salvation.

Some televised preachers present messages which are pure speculation and some are mouthpieces of other preachers, seemingly not having confirmed for themselves through God's Word what they are conveying. Thus any of us can fall into a trap if we believe everything we hear without running it by God's Word first as per counsel, especially if it is quoted as being a revelation of the Lord. Such case is presented in the Bible regarding a prophet who directly received specific instructions from God to not take a certain path when returning to his home. Then a second prophet told him he had received directions from God and the Lord wanted him to indeed take the path he had intentions of not taking. Though the declaration contradicted the first prophet's initial instructions, yet he believed the lie and went the way in which the Lord had revealed to him that he should not go. That prophet died that very day, for on that road there was a lion which killed him. (1 King 13) That narration ought to shake us right out of our boots.

Therefore, because Scripture counsels us to know God's Spirit, (1 John 4:2) and His Spirit will direct us because we are also God's children, we must seek to be in tune with the Comforter, as He will give us peace that surpasses all understanding when we make choices which are agreeable with God's will for us. If we have feelings of unrest, it may not be God's will. However, if we do have God's peace and act, *but then* we experience unrest, know that God's warning comes *before* and not after the fact, and that uneasiness may be the enemy trying to sow doubt in your heart.

We are to pray for our pastors and render to them the consideration they deserve as human beings. Also knowing that God has allowed them to be in the position they are holding, we are to respect them, for David also honored King Saul. Yet Scripture admonishes us to validate their teachings, retaining that which is good. And we should heed their counsel only if it concurs with God's will for us, especially if we had prior confirmation from the Holy Spirit and are personally convicted of God's guidance. "Prove all things; hold fast that which is good." (1 Thessalonians 5:21)

Some renown preachers who have healing ministries at times give irrational directions to follow (*not necessarily* in sending them money but sometimes that too) as a prerequisite to obtaining a miracle or blessing. Although there are some Biblical narrations which required that a person obey certain directions as the criterion for God to heal them, nonetheless, a study of them will reveal a powerful spiritual lesson which even we may apply to our daily Christian walk. However, if puzzling directions are taken right out of thin air, beware, because such manner of conditions are also dictated in occult religions as prerequisites for favors attributed to God.

I had the opportunity to chat with a young man who, traveling cross-country, stopped in a town in Texas. A "man of God" there told him that he had received instructions from God about him, and the young man was to translate into Spanish all the works of that man. The young man told me that immediately he felt repulsion for the words, for God had not instructed him (the young man himself) concerning the matter. He was also surprised to meet many persons who honored the words of that man and did as they were counseled. After a short visit the young man left Waco and continued on his way, never acting upon the instructions of David Koresh.

I recall when I was in elementary school our class was in the chapel and our teacher, a nun, pointed to a book on the altar. She told us it was a sin for us to read it, for it could only be read by priests and even they could only read it during mass. I did not know what book it was, but that happened to be my introduction to the Bible—it has not been that many years since the Catholic church began lifting its ban on God's Word. Immediately I made a determination that when I grew up I was going to read that book and find out for myself what was it, that it said, that I was not supposed to know. But I just could not wait it out. Therefore, at a time when no one was around, I entered the chapel, headed for the altar and took the Bible. It was in Latin, but of course. What a disappointment! But thinking that the nuns who prepared the meals did not know what our teacher told us, I headed for the kitchen which was off limits to the students. Yet I entered the restricted area, and lifting the Book up to the first nun I saw, opened It at random and pointed, "Could you tell me what it says here?" She was scandalized and made me place It back on the altar.

After that, my teacher, who was no Mother Theresa, every time she passed me on the hallway and no one was around, would slap me. One time, as she was approaching, I saw her smile which had fooled me repeatedly. So as we passed each other, I ducked. It just so happened that on that one occasion we were on the second floor hallway and passed each other right at the top landing of a wide and beautiful, marble staircase which winded down onto the lobby. The strength she had put into the blow was such that its force thrust her off balance when she missed here target, me, and had she not instinctively gone for the handrail and grabbed it firmly, she would have tumbled down the staircase. Coming up from my squat position I turned my head for an instant and got a glimpse of her wild maneuvering but never stopped walking away. I believe that when timing is perfect, God is in the manner, and He did take care of me perfectly, for she never attempted to slap me again. When I became an adult, I bought my very own Bible and it changed my life and that of my parents. However, I have always wondered, What about the rest of the students? Did some hold fast to her instructions?

And what about what our children are learning? One of my sons came home from school one day and told me his teacher proposed this paradox: If God is so powerful that He can create anything, can He then create a stone that He Himself cannot move? If He cannot create it, He is not God. But if He creates it, but cannot move it, still He is not God. The question is designed to destroy faith. The school was a public school which bans promoting God, but apparently does not ban targeting Him. The question took me by surprise and I asked my son to give me time to pray about it.

The Bible gave me the answer. Our heart is that stone. God granted His creation freedom of choice, though His desire is to "remove from them their heart of stone and give them a heart of flesh." (Ezekiel 11:19) But in order that we may live experiencing true, authentic freedom, God voluntarily barred Himself. However, in His refraining to act for the sake of our liberty, He effectuated a greater and more beautiful solution. He turned His power to move the stone into a promise that is at our disposal should we wish for Him to move it.

Though that paradox came from a secular environment, targets of doubt and shady procedures come from all angles including Christian settings. Thus we are to ponder upon and pray about what we are told, rather than concede to sarcastic remarks or serious teachings at face value. Within a religious atmosphere, some speakers even go as far as requesting that the congregation close their eyes and imagine Jesus is talking to them, and they guide them through visualizations while emphasizing that they heed the words which Jesus is whispering into their mind. However, all of that is speculation because "No eye has seen, no ear has heard, no mind has conceived what God has prepared for those who love him." (1 Corinthians 2:9, NIV; see also Isaiah 64:4) Further, God already spoke to us and put His Word in writing, into Holy Scripture, and should He wish to speak to us further, He will do so at the moment He determines, not when someone tells us that He will.

One thing is to listen as someone prays lifting their voice in supplication, or when we receive counsel and are told, "think about it," meaning that at some time when we decide to, we will consider the matter to reason it out; and another thing is to actually accept to think what we are told to think at a specific moment, for it is then that we are virtually surrendering our thought process to another for them to control us as they guide us as to what to visualize. The latter is precisely a hypnotic tool that creates the perfect setup for the influence of another voice, but which the speaker is telling us is Jesus. Dangerous! Another exemplary formula used to control the minds is first proposing to the congregation a complex, incongruous questions that the minds needs to resolve. It serves to stun the listeners momentarily and jolts the mind into a pause mode that gives the speaker a chance to get his foot in the door to our subconscious. As the audience allows these situations, their minds are guided with soft vocal tones that may become monotone. When the speaker wants to end the control, he will firm up his tone and speak louder and faster. That is the equivalent of the clap of the hands to break a hypnotic spell. Numerous are the methods Satan uses in his battle for the control of the minds, individually and of the masses, hence the responsibility that we are to set our eyes on God and no other, being sober at all times. (1 Peter 1:13)

There is a tale about a man who every morning passed a jewelry store which had in front of it on the sidewalk a big clock on a pole. The man would pause, check his pocket watch and set it accordingly, then continued on his way. The owner of the jewelry store was so intrigued by the fellow, that one morning he waited for him to inquire who he was. It turned out the man worked at a nearby factory and one of his duties included activating the quitting siren. Wanting to always be fair with his coworkers, he took the precaution of every morning making sure his watch was accurate. The store owner, amazed, confessed, "I set this clock every evening when I hear the siren." So also we may have the best of intentions, yet do not realize that by looking at each other as guides, we will always be off a little or a lot. We cannot behold each other and accept whatever comes along without investigating the origin of procedures, formats and teachings.

My first full time job was as a bank teller. During my first week I asked if there were any samples of counterfeit money, that I may see the difference. My trainer told me that if I only look at authentic money, then, when a counterfeit is handed over to me, immediately I would recognize it. That is what happened. Months later, a woman handed me $50 in five dollar bills. By that time I counted money very fast. And, without skipping a beat, I counted aloud, "5, 10, 15, counterfeit, 20, 25, 30, 35, 40, 45." I did not hesitate while counting, and as I said, "counterfeit," I placed that bill apart from the stack, but keeping the same fast pace as if all the bills had been authentic. And, as soon as I said, "45," I picked it up, "Ma'am, I'm sorry, but this is a counterfeit and I cannot return it to you." I viewed that bill in a jiffy, but recognized it instantly as a counterfeit because I had only been looking at real money. Likewise, we can recognize false doctrines right away if we continually learn more and more from Scripture by beholding only Truth. But if we neglect to study the Original and instead behold more and more one another, we will not be able to discern when we are handed a counterfeit teaching, doctrine or advice, or are ushered into questionable rituals and practices. Likewise, knowing the Original helps us abandon, modify or affirm teachings and doctrines, as well as practices which we already uphold, thus molding us into being in harmony with Scripture.

When my oldest son graduated from boot camp, I attended the wonderful and memorable ceremony outdoors, and sat along with the other families and friends in the bleachers. Different companies marched on the field, each group formed into rows and columns of uniformed servicemen/women. They approached the bleachers from our left and passed in front of us while their heads turned towards the audience acknowledging us. We returned the courtesy by applauding each company that passed by. And I was in awe, because they each kept perfect, identical distance from each other, though their heads were turned to their right looking at us as they marched forward. How could they do that, keep order moving forward while looking to the right? It was not until a few companies had passed, that it dawned on me that the first column of marchers, the column closest to the bleachers, had not turned their heads, but in fact where still gazing straight ahead watching where they were going. The rest of those in the company, though they seemed to be looking at us, because their heads were turned in our direction, in reality were not looking at the audience. Rather, each one had their eyes set on one of the marchers in the first column, and used that person as their point of reference and guide. That was the trick to their keeping perfect order. So also we march in truth only when we gaze straight ahead looking at our Leader, Christ. And if someone counsels us or teaches us, then we are to prove where that person's eyes are set. Are they looking at Jesus? For that reason, as per counsel, the reader must prove this book, and then retain the good.

Yet, before closing this chapter, I would like to suggest that whenever Christians meet, whether only a few persons in a private home, at the church service, or thousands attending a convention, that we set aside a *minimum* of five minutes for every hour that the gathering takes place, and divide in groups of two, three or four with the persons near us, and pray for ourselves and our children. An all-day gathering could include two or three of those powerful prayer times lasting ten to fifteen minutes each. These would be in addition to the scheduled prayers by the coordinators and presenters of the event. However, by the end of the event, those times when the congregation prays in groups, would have totaled only 30 to 45 minutes if we hold three such small sessions. This would not be unreasonable considering that on the eve of His death Jesus requested his disciples to pray and keep watch for at least one hour. "Sit here while I go over there and pray... My soul is deeply grieved, to the point of death, remain here and keep watch with Me... You could not keep watch with me one hour? Keep watching and praying, that you may not enter into temptation." (Matthew 26:36, 38, 40-41)

12

Casting Out Demons

Some preachers, while delivering their sermon, mock Satan or address him by name. There are people who also suggest that during our prayer time we should address Satan by name and order him to leave. Others claim they do that at home each morning. Is it because Satan is right there with them that they talk to him? There is not one verse in the model prayer Jesus taught us that includes such conduct. Jesus never mocked Satan or enjoyed ridiculing him. And Jesus only addressed the enemy when Satan openly manifested himself first. The Old Testament bans us from going to places where spirits are invoked. (Leviticus 19:26, 31; Deuteronomy 18:10-12, 14) In those places, men communicate with Satan and his angels directly when those evil spirits disguise themselves as persons who have passed away. Shall we disobey God and while in the sanctity of our home or from the pulpit address Satan, even mock him to his face so to speak, or order him out even though there is no palpable manifestation of the evil one? Doing so would be equivalent to going to a place of divination to communicate with demonic spirits. The only difference is that by doing it wherever we are at, we take a short cut and instead invite Satan over by the mere act of speaking to him directly, in the second person.

Yet, some folk who are said to be in ministry casting out demons from people who are demon possessed, establish conversations with the fallen angels inquiring of them to find out how they work. But are not those evil spirits liars? Why do we need to learn anything from them? Is not the Word of God good enough for us? Jesus addressed Satan only when Satan addressed Jesus first openly. Jesus never went out of His way to talk to demons and those who dare do so enter into demonic territory at their own risk. God has never sanctioned that practice.

Even Paul never did that. In a passage we quoted earlier, about a damsel possessed with a spirit of divination, we note that it was not until *many days* had passed that finally Paul could not bear her any longer and addressed the spirit in the name of Jesus, casting it out of her. (Acts 16:16-18) But Paul did not establish a conversation with the spirit.

Further, among us there may be believers whose minds may be very susceptible. How are we to know how they may be affected if we fall into the practice of addressing demons just because? In particular, this could be devastating to children whose tender minds may be the most vulnerable. What if they or those who are of weak faith begin to imitate the practice and start to talk to Satan directly, even mocking him? Would not that be giving occasion to Satan to actually come and hang around? The impressionable minds of those tender in the faith are prone to be defenseless, while children, lacking the power of reason, may become the target of the evil one's snares if they start talking to Satan. But even those who are strong in the faith, inclusive of a speaker addressing the devil, by so doing they make themselves accessible to him.

An impacting Bible passage relates a brief dialog between Jesus and a demonic. "For he said unto him, Come out of the man, thou unclean spirit. And he asked him, What is thy name? And he answered, saying, My name is Legion: for we are many." (Mark 5:8-9; see also Luke 8:30) Are we part of a legion? Have we yielded to a "group mentality?" It is dangerous to sacrifice our own individuality, whether in religion, politics, or a social setting. We have the privilege of choosing to have our mindset in the Lord, and we should not be lazy about exercising our right and duty. Let us follow the Shepherd, not the herd.

Understanding this issue, I refrain from even singing the enemy's name which a few hymns may include. And that is why I am keeping this chapter as short as possible.

13

LOVE AND TONGUES

Love will last forever, but tongues one day will end. That truth is expressed in an all-time favorite Bible chapter, 1 Corinthians 13. Because the contrast between these two subjects was addressed by Paul, it would seem appropriate to discuss herein the vital one: Love.

In the beginning God created the heavens and the earth, and the earth was without form and void. (Genesis 1) Sometimes I imagine that when God planned the creation of man, before it actually took place and at the very moment He first conceived it, it may have gone something like this:

God planned, "On the first day, there will be light." At that very moment light from His throne obeyed and began to travel to planet earth. "On the second day I will separate the waters, and on the third day I will cause the dry land to appear." And light from His throne continued to travel to our planet. God planned the fourth day, the fifth day, the sixth day... and light continued to travel our way.

"I will crown the work of creation on the sixth day by creating man, male and female, in our image, in the image of God." Looking into the future, God knew man would sin against Him. But He also saw that there was hope of salvation if His son, Jesus, would trade places with man. The time was the foundation of the world and the moment for a solemn decision. Would the Son of God die for man?

Looking ahead at fallen man, Jesus had pity on us; and His voice was lifted as if reaching out to humanity, who had not yet been created, to tell us that we could have hope because He loved us. There was urgency in His voice. Jesus was anxious to start the ball rolling that He may experience Calvary for our sake. His eagerness to die for mankind was made evident when throughout the whole universe the thunder of His voice was heard as He shouted the testimony of His love: "Let there be light!"

At that very moment, the light arrived. Just like it will be someday when there will be no need of light from the sun or the moon, because our world will be illuminated with the light of the Lord Almighty and the Lamb, (Revelation 21:23) so also that first day was a unique day when our planet shone with light from God's throne. The heart of God was glad. The first step in the plan was now in effect, and God saw that it was good.

Just as foreseen by God, man sinned. (Genesis 3) Adam and Eve did not ask to be saved. Regardless, God made a promise of salvation anyway. It was His pleasure to do so. And the promise was pronounced even before the first couple was cursed.

Later, when Eve had her first son she said, "God has given me a male child." (Genesis 4:1) Upon gladly acknowledging God's will for her, Eve gave evidence of her submissiveness to God. We see this again after Abel's death. She gave birth to Seth and said, "God has given me a male child in the place of Abel, whom Cain killed. And Seth also had a son. Then the people began to turn to the Lord." (Genesis 4:25-26) Notice the order of events. Eve acknowledged that God gave her Seth in place of Abel. Later Seth had his own son and it was then that the people began to turn to the Lord. Eve did not curse God for the death of Abel. She could have said, "Why did God allow this tragedy to happen to me?" Instead, she expressed gratitude for yet another son, thus giving testimony that her heart was tender toward God. I believe that Eve raised Seth in a special way, in the fear of the Lord; and when Seth had his own son, he then put together the natural love he was experiencing with the words of faith his mother taught him, and thus it was that Seth came to understand the love of God. As a consequence, he must have become an evangelist, for the Bible says that it was then that the people began to turn to the Lord. But though Eve may have worked for God's cause in the preparation of her son, if Seth had been the promised one, then it could be said that the promise of God was fulfilled partly due to Eve's helping out in the matter. So the promise was fulfilled 4000 years later, so that all would know that Eve had nothing to do with its fulfillment. It was God Who made the promise, though Adam and Eve had not asked to be saved, and God alone would fulfill it.

The years passed and the promise was repeated to Abraham. (Genesis 15) Sarah was to have a child, but so that she would not be credited with the fulfillment of the promise, Isaac was not born until well after the time that Sarah was too old to bear children. Thus we know that God alone fulfilled the promise that He made.

The children of Israel were promised that after four hundred years of bondage they would be delivered out of Egypt. (*Ibid*., 15:13) If Moses had inherited the throne of Pharaoh, it would seem as if God needed someone in a position of authority to free Israel; and so it was that Moses lost his right to the throne, (Exodus 2) that we may know God had the power of fulfilling His own promise, regardless of the position Moses held.

God promised to take the children of Israel into a land of milk and honey. (*Ibid*., chap. 3) Moses, in a moment of desperation because of Israel's unbelief, stated, "Must we fetch you water out of this rock?" (Numbers 20:10) Moses included himself in the miracles. "Must *we*...." If Moses were allowed to live and enter with Israel into Canaan, it would appear that Moses had in fact been partly responsible for the miracles, and that the Israelites would be able to enter Canaan only because of Moses' leadership. Therefore, Moses was taken out of the way, and we have as a testimony that without Moses the children of Israel still entered the promised land, for all the miracles they received were from God alone, Who was guiding and protecting them in fulfillment of His goodwill toward them demonstrated via His own promise which they never even asked for.

When Israel was bordering Canaan for the first time, there were two men of faith, Joshua and Caleb. They claimed that by God's Spirit in them they would conquer the giants in the land. (*Ibid.*, chap. 13-14) Moses believed, but not so the people. Thus came God's verdict to Israel to go back into the wilderness. (*Ibid.*, 14:31-35) The giants of Canaan were representative of our sins. (*Education*, p. 150) Our tendency to sin is a great giant before us and we need to conquer it. How can we do it? David, as a youth, believed that he could conquer the giant Goliath and he did conquer. (1 Samuel 17) We must also believe that we can conquer the menacing giant of our inclination to sin which is before us, because that is the Gospel. That is why Jesus came, to save his people *from* their sins. (Matthew 1:21)

When people are trapped in a burning building, firemen either save them *from* the fire, or abandon them *in* the fire. Firemen cannot save people by leaving them *in* the fire. Jesus did not come to save us *in* our sins. We are either saved, rescued, delivered, freed *from* sin, or we are abandoned *in* sin, but never saved *in* sin. Saved *in* sin is a contradiction. It is nonexistent. It is a mental delusion. It is an insult to intelligence.

Jesus came to save his people *from* their sins. That is the Good News. That is what salvation is all about. It is a promise, and, just as we have seen, God fulfills all of His promises. The promise is found in Ezekiel 36:26-27, 31. It reads:

> *I will give you a new heart and put a new spirit within you; I will take the heart of stone out of your flesh and give*

you a heart of flesh. I will put My Spirit [Capital S] within you and cause you to walk in My statutes, and you will keep My judgments and do them... Then you will remember your evil ways and your deeds that were not good; and you will loathe yourselves in your own sight, for your iniquities and your abominations. (NKJV)

How are we to conquer? Let us follow the example of David. David conquered Goliath by first going to the stream. (1 Samuel 17:40) We must then go to the river of life, to the throne of God. At the stream David chose unique stones. (Ibid. 17:40) At the throne of God we must choose the unique Rock, Jesus. David's stone injured the giant in the forehead. (vs. 49) Our Rock, Jesus, has already bruised the serpent's head. (Genesis 3:15) And David, filled with the Spirit of the Lord, ran to the defeated giant, and, as the Spanish translation states it, David "finished killing him." (1 Samuel 17:51) Likewise, the Spirit of the Lord in us will finish sin off for us. That is a promise, "I will put my Spirit within you, and cause you to walk in my statutes." When we walk in His statutes, we do not transgress His law. Sin is the transgression of the law. (1 John 3:4) Therefore, the only solution to our not sinning is the Spirit of God in us.

Jesus showed us how it works. He was filled with the Holy Spirit (Luke 4:1) and did not sin. (Hebrews 4:15) If the Spirit of God were also in us, our faith would be like the faith of Jesus, obedient to the commandments of God and filled with works of mercy for all of humanity. Jesus went about doing good, healing the sick, comforting the broken-hearted.

"I saw that it is in the providence of God that widows and orphans, the blind, the deaf, the lame, and persons afflicted in a variety of ways, have been placed in close Christian relationship with His church; it is to prove His people and develop their true character. Angels of God are watching to see how we treat these persons who need our sympathy, love, and disinterested benevolence. This is God's test of our character... Those who have pity for ... the needy, Christ represents as commandment keepers, who shall have eternal life." (*3 Testimony to the Church*, pp. 511-512)

Why does Jesus represents those who express love by acts of mercy as commandment keepers? Because upon love hangs the Law of God. (Matthew 22:37-40) We must realize that the Gospel is providing for our fellowmen who are unfortunate. His angels are ministering spirits. (Matthew 4:1; Mark 1:13; Psalms 91:11) The kingdom of God, then, is a kingdom of service. This is because the kingdom of God is a kingdom of love, a kingdom of grace. Grace is to do a favor, a service. We are under His grace in that He wants to do us the favor of giving us His Spirit so that we may have power to do His will, which is expressed in His law. He loves us. And true love is charity, that is, giving without expecting anything in return. Charity is expressed in service. God is serving us by giving us His Spirit. In turn we must do the same and serve humanity. Jesus said that whosoever is willing to be a servant shall be great in the kingdom of God. (Matthew 23:11) And the more we serve, the greater we are in a kingdom of service which is a kingdom of charity, that is, a kingdom of love, and, hence, it is the kingdom of God.

Listening to the Word awakens faith in us. Seeing others live the Gospel inspires us. But it is not until we ourselves go out of our way and make an effort to provide for others, that we are actually transformed. Just like exercise transforms us physically, love (charity). in action transforms us spiritually. The more we serve, the more we love, and "love shall cover a multitude of sins." (1 Peter 4:8)

We will never get anywhere if we just listen to the Gospel, but do not live the Gospel. That is why it is called, the "living" Gospel. We may believe that a gymnasium has the power to transform us physically, but it does us no good if we do not use it. The homeless, the prisoners, the sick, the singles, the lonely of all ages, the aged, the widows, the orphans, the single parents, and suffering humanity at large, are our gymnasium. We are to exercise our spiritual muscles in the gymnasium of human beings who need many things from us, starting with a simple smile. Then it is that we will be transformed into the likeness of He who provides for everyone.

A good marital relationship does not depend on each side contributing 50%, but rather on both the husband and the wife each contributing 100%. It is the same with the relationship we are to have with God. He is our Husband and we are His bride. (Isaiah 54:5) My brothers and sisters, God contributes 100% in His plan to save us. Now it is our turn, as His bride, to contribute our 100% and make an effort to cooperate with Him in the spiritual realm just as we make an effort to exercise in pro of health in the physical realm.

The Bible says that demons also believe. (James 2:19-20) But what is the difference between our faith and the faith of demons? Demons do not love, and if we do not love one another either, there is no difference. If we are able to serve but do not, there is no difference. If we continue to live without having the works of charity for one another, there is no difference. "Faith without works is dead." (*Ibid.*, 2:20) If we are ashamed of even speaking to an unfortunate soul, there is no difference. If we gossip about someone—and gossip is a clear evidence that we do not love that person—there is no difference. We might as well accept the title of demon, because we believe, but do not love.

Would you dare declare to someone openly, in public, and for all to clearly hear: "You are the Son of God!"? It takes more than just faith to do that. You may be convicted that your friend *is* the Son of God, but you will *not* declare it publicly unless you are driven by an ardent, fervent, passionate element that moves you to declare it, if need be, in the presence of the whole world, and without being a bit ashamed. That element is love.

Love is what moved one of the thieves crucified along with Christ. While others were mocking Jesus, the thief did not see a dying man next to him because the eyes of love made him behold a Savior as he implored, "Lord, remember me!" (Luke 23:42) Tortured and about to die, Jesus had heard no one, not even His disciples, address Him as "Lord." It was love that tore from the criminal's heart the words acknowledging Jesus' divinity. Love is what causes a man to stand at the altar and declare to the world that he has prepared a pedestal in his heart for the woman he is marrying. Love can move a mountain!

This kind of love is what gave Peter the impulse to confess in public to Jesus, "You are the Son of God!" Jesus discerned Peter's love for Him and replied: "Upon this rock I will build my church" (Matthew 16:18). Yes. Love is the rock upon which is built God's church, and we positively know this, that Jesus was talking about love as the Rock and not Peter as the Rock, because Peter himself tells us so in his epistle. Jesus is "the living stone... chosen of God, and precious." (1 Peter 2:4) It was the love expressed and made evident by Peter's statement at that moment that constituted the Rock upon which is built God's church. Peter tells us that the Rock is Jesus. (*Ibid.*, 2:4) We know that Jesus is God. (Romans 9:5). The Spanish version translates that verse clearly: "Jesus, who is God over all things." We also know that God is love. (1 John 4:8) Therefore, if the Rock is Jesus, and Jesus is God, and God is love, then *the Rock is love*. Upon love is built God's church!

After Peter betrayed Jesus, our Lord took Peter back to the issue that made Peter fall. Jesus did not ask, "Peter, what happened to your faith?" or "What happened to your trust?" or "What happened to your leadership?" as if Peter had been placed in a position superior to his brethren. No. Jesus instead took Peter back to the issue of love, which was the very point where Peter failed, for Jesus basically asked him, "Peter, what happened to your love?" when He asked him *three* times, "Peter, *do you love me*?" (John 21:15-17) Love was the Rock manifested by Peter and Jesus ushered Peter back unto Love.

At the moment that Peter had confessed in public that Jesus was the Son of God, Jesus did not set Peter aside for a special work of leadership because of that open confession. The Kingdom of God is not built upon Peter, for man is not the foundation of Heaven. It is the spiritual ingredient of love that Peter manifested which Jesus upheld, and in no way was Jesus shifting His divinity unto Peter. However, later on Jesus did say that it was the Comforter, the Holy Spirit, the One Who would be taking His place, for God's divine authority can only be carried out by One Who is also Divine. (John 16:7)

The idea of Peter bearing authority over his brethren further tumbles when we consider the following. On the very last day in which our Lord was literally on this earth, and immediately after His ascension, Peter attributed to himself the discretion of choosing an apostle to fill the place left vacant by Judas. (Acts 1:15-26) Later on Jesus *personally* chose Paul. (Acts 9:1-16) And Paul called himself an apostle[18] and safeguards his position as such. (1 Corinthians 9:1, 2; 15:9-10; 1 Timothy 2:7; 2 Timothy 1:11) In the New Jerusalem there will be inscribed the names of the twelve apostles. (Revelation 21:14) Judas' name will not be there because he abandoned his call. So whose name will fill that vacant spot? If it is the name of the man chosen by Peter, then that renders Peter's action above the Lord's, even though Peter was not even sure of who should fill Judas' place out of two candidates he selected, neither of which was heard of after that. If it is the name of the man personally chosen by Jesus, that is, Paul, who stands out and shines throughout the New Testament, then that renders Peter as starting off on the wrong foot. There is only space for one name. Will the true apostle please stand up?

Since an apostle is one *personally* chosen by Jesus, Peter's hurried action in fulfilling the prophesy from Psalm 109:8 comes

---

18 See the first verse in each of Romans, 1 Corinthians, 2 Corinthians, Galatians, Ephesians, Colossians, 1 Timothy, 2 Timothy and Titus.

across as pretentious and conclusively renders him fallible. That makes a powerful statement for those of us who act according to what we think is God's purpose, without consulting God's will in the matter or whether the timing for it is apropos. Consequently, we too usurp the rank that belongs only to the Divine when we act out our will and not God's. Yet we were not left as orphans, for Christ's representative on earth, the Holy Spirit, is our Guide sent by the Father to be always with us, even until the end of time. (John 14:16, 26; 15:26; 16:7)

Consequently, in His statement to Peter, Jesus dealt with the real issue at hand as soon as Peter acknowledged that Jesus was the Son of God. And the issue was *love*, for love is the ultimate goal, and greater than faith. (1 Corinthians 13:13) I may have faith that, if you are sick, my visit can be like a healing ointment, but love is the driving force which causes me to visit you. So through faith we accept that which is truth, and through love we follow through with our faith and live for God. Faith causes us to believe the Gospel. Love turns it into the "living" Gospel. And since love is charity, (vs. 1) and charity is expressed in works of mercy, then true faith is expressed in works. James, the brother of Jesus, said it clearly: "Show me your faith without works, and I will show you my faith by my works... faith without works is dead." (James 2:18–20) Love is the ingredient that makes faith come to life. That is why love is greater than faith.

A scribe understood the supremacy of love and told Jesus that he understood that love for God and for our neighbors is more valuable than burnt offerings and sacrifices. (Mark 12:32-33) Jesus, seeing this man's understanding, answered, "You are not far from the kingdom of God." (vs. 34) That is it! If we, likewise, are able to grasp that understanding, that love for each other is supreme, we shall also be *not far* from the kingdom of God. But being not far is not good enough. Someday the wicked will be not far from the New Jerusalem. (Revelation 20:7-9)

Jesus visited the tax collector, Zaccheus. And Zaccheus said, "Behold, Lord, the half of my goods I give to the poor; and if I have taken any thing from any man by false accusation, I restore him fourfold." (Luke 19:8) We notice Zaccheus did not only understand; he was going to follow through according to his understanding. He said, "I will give to the poor. I will restore fourfold." Zaccheus was going to have *works*. Hearing this, Jesus testified, "This day is salvation come to this house." (vs. 9) Therefore, Zaccheus did not just get to be not far from the kingdom. Because his faith was a faith that upholds the works of love, he actually had the kingdom of God enter into his home!

The young man who visited Jesus had one thing missing. It seemed that he had never cared for the poor. (Matthew 19:16-22) He knew the law of the kingdom, but had never lived the kingdom in service to others. But the actual words Jesus used were, "If you want to be perfect, go, sell all your possessions and give the money to the poor." (vs. 21) Why? Because perfect love gives it all, like God's love. God gave it all. It was the Father Himself who guided His people during Old Testament times. But just like Adam and Eve had done at the beginning rejecting God, Israel also rejected the Father and chose a king. Having rejected the Father, still our sins could be forgiven, because God would send His Son. But we killed God's Son. We rejected God's gift of eternal life. Having murdered Jesus, still our sins could be forgiven, because God would send His Holy Spirit, our final hope of salvation. But if we reject the Holy Spirit our sins cannot be forgiven, not because the Holy Spirit is of greater esteem than the Father or the Son, not because God is not willing to forgive us, but because when we reject the Holy Spirit, then we have shunned each person of the Trinity and heaven has no more to offer that we may be rescued from sin.

But let us not reject God's Spirit. Rather, let us claim the promise, "I will put my Spirit within you, and cause you to walk in my statutes." (Ezekiel 36:27) Jesus said in Luke 11:11-13: "If a son shall ask bread of any of you that is a father, will he give him a stone? or if he ask a fish, will he for a fish give him a serpent? Or if he shall ask an egg, will he offer him a scorpion? If ye then, being evil, know how to give good gifts unto your children; how much more shall your heavenly Father give the Holy Spirit *to them that ask him*?" God will not violate our free will and give us something we do not want. The Bible plainly states that God's Spirit will be given "*to them that ask him.*" We must ask for His Spirit.

Through God's Spirit in us we will see in our lives the words of Jesus recorded in Matthew 5:40-48. "If a man... take away thy coat, let him have thy cloak also." In other words, we will always be willing to keep giving. "And whosoever shall compel thee to go a mile, go with him two." We will always be willing to do a favor. "Love your enemies, bless them that curse you, do good to them." We will have no resentment or hate in our hearts, thus Jesus sums it all up by concluding: "Be ye therefore perfect, even as your Father which is in heaven is perfect." In other words, we will always be giving, caring, with love in our hearts, so that our love may also be like God's love, a perfect, neverending love.

After we give it all, if we are stabbed in the back, what then? Many will be discouraged and will not want to help anyone else again. Jesus knew this would happen, and therefore said, "And because iniquity shall abound, the love of many shall wax cold." (Matthew 24:12) But we must continue to serve regardless, because Jesus added in the following verse, "But he that shall endure unto the end, the same shall be saved." Notice, he said, "the love of many shall wax cold, but he that shall endure unto the end..." Endure in what? Endure in love, in charity, in service, in grace, in favors to needy humanity, the same shall be saved.

Let us continue to give service even after getting stabbed in the back, so that our love may be perfect, perfect because it will not wax cold, will never die, like God's love. But, can we possibly love everybody? A young woman shared with me a guilty feeling that haunted her. She met her husband at a time when he was separated from his first wife, with whom he had a child, and they possibly could get back together. She felt that if it had not been because of her, his first marriage would still have had a chance. Then after she was married to him and had children with him, she met Jesus, and since then felt guilty. She asked me, "Will God ever forgive me?"

I answered, "My story is the same as yours, except that in my case, I am the first wife. And when I went to speak with the other woman and I said to her, 'I love my husband.' She replied with arrogance, 'I love him, too.' My children at that time were 4, 5 and 6 years old.

"From that day on, every day I knelt beside my bed with my eyes opened and my arms stretched up to heaven as if grabbing God to make sure He was paying attention—you know those times of urgency praying—and I sincerely told God what was in my heart. I shouted, 'I hate her! I hate her! What are you going to do about it? How can you save us both? What's your trick? Because heaven is not big enough for the two of us there!'

"Three years went by and I saw her again in church the day two of my children were getting baptized. Now, she was the wife. And a force drove me to walk up to her, extend my hand to greet her with a handshake, and I said, 'Thank you for coming, and thank you for treating my children so well.' She was stunned. And I was stunned, too, because I was sincere. I went to the secretary's office to cry. And I cried because of happiness, because God had removed the burden of hate from my heart. The past was forgotten. I was free, and I am still free from that hate.

"A year later she had her first child, and I bought her son a present. A neighbor of mine asked me, 'How can you do that? The same thing happened to me five years before it happened to you, and to this day I still cannot stand the sight of that other woman.'

I told my neighbor what happened. God performed His trick. He circumcised the hate from my heart, miraculously. I don't know how He did it or when He did it. But He did it."

And I further said to that young woman, "If you were to see us talking, you would never guess that there had been something wrong at one time, and you would not detect any resentment, because there is none. God forgave her, but allowed His forgiveness to also be channeled through my heart so that I may experience a hint of God's love." And I added, "Don't worry about it anymore. God has forgiven you. Throw away the guilt and from now on live for God."

Such forgiveness which God made me capable of offering is but a glimpse of what God has done with all of us. He has forgiven us. Let us accept His forgiveness, throw away the guilt, and from now on live for Him. Let us give Him all of our feelings, so that He can turn them all into love. God's circumcision of the heart is perfect and not only does He have the power to perform miracles in our hearts, but He wants to perform the miracle of giving us a new heart, a heart that loves, a new spirit, a spirit that is submissive to His will, a spirit that forgives those who hurt us, as God forgives.

I am not presenting here a concept categorized as a new doctrine of "holy flesh." Rather, I am reminding of an old promise of Holy Spirit. Sin causes us to have a spirit that hates and is resentful. The Holy Spirit will transform it into a spirit that loves. And I am speaking about charity. Charity means using the spiritual gymnasium God has provided for us. "Above all things have fervent charity among yourselves: for charity shall cover the multitude of sins." (1 Peter 4:8)

Years ago, I was asked at church to deliver a basket of food to a needy couple who had four children. The youngest child had a special device surgically implanted into his windpipe, so that at night the mother would connect oxygen to it. This boy's case had made the headlines in our city's newspaper and the news reached the White House at the time Ronald Reagan was president. Mr. Reagan wanted to speak to the mother, but the family had no telephone. She told me that the White House called the hospital at the time she had just left for home. So the White House ordered the telephone company to install a telephone in her home. When she got to the house, the telephone was working; it rang, she answered it, and spoke to the President of the United States. The man in authority, all the way from Washington, D.C. used the power he had, and the problem was resolved. But the mother had to choose to answer the telephone and speak to President Reagan.

Brothers and sisters, our love lines are out-of-order. But the Man in authority wants to reconnect those vital lines, severed because we choose to sin. God promised He would do it and, as we have beheld, He will fulfill His promise. The heart of Jesus is filled with love. His love comes to us through the Holy Spirit, because the Holy Spirit is God, and God is love. But we must choose whether or not to open the door of our heart for Jesus to enter so that His Spirit may abide in us, cast out our eternal death sentence, and fit us to live with God. Jesus gladly gave up His life to die for us. Now it is our turn to give up our eternal death to live for Him. What a bargain! If we do not respond, it is because we are nothing more than fools.

Are you tired of resentment? Would you like to have the power of love to overcome hate, bitterness and all manner of wickedness? His love will motivate you to follow through according to your faith. It will turn the Gospel into a living Gospel in your life and bring you peace. In the beginning Jesus was eager to start the ball rolling to save us when He declared, "let there be light." Are you eager to start the ball rolling in giving Him your heart? If so, then now is your turn to say, "let there be light."

God is love. "He that loveth not knoweth not God, for God is love." (1 John 4:8) Heaven's ultimate goal is restoring God's image in us. That is why when we consider the meaning of love versus the meaning of having the gift of tongues, we may understand Paul's words in 1 Corinthians 13. Hence, if I speak tongues and have not love, I am only making noise. If I understand all prophecy and even publish a book titled *TONGUES Dissecting the Gift* where all may get an idea I have some Bible knowledge, but have not love, I am nothing. And if I die a martyr for righteousness sake, but have not love, it does me no good. Dear reader, What do you desire more, love or tongues? The answer ought to be that which has eternal consequences. Love will last forever. Tongues one day will end. (1 Corinthians 13:8)

14

WOMEN AT CORINTH

> **1 Corinthians 14:34-35** *"Let the women keep silence in the churches: for it is not permitted unto them to speak; but they are commanded to be under obedience, as also saith the law... for it is a shame for women to speak in the church."*

These verses are only a piece of a jigsaw puzzle, the others being other Biblical accounts regarding women as instruments in the plan of salvation. Viewing only one piece does not enable us to see the total picture. On the day of Pentecost Peter explained the events of that day by quoting a prophecy foretelling a work to be done by both men and women, "your sons and your daughters will prophesy." (Act 2:17-18; Joel 2:28-29 Since "to prophesy" means "to preach," then, in order for that to occur, a person must speak. Further, it was the Holy Spirit that gave them utterance. Prior to that day, Scripture also gives accounts of women judges and prophetesses. (Exodus 15:20; 2 Kings 22:14; 2 Chronicles 34:22; Nehemiah 6:14; Isaiah 8:3)

With this in mind, these instructions by Paul seem inconsistent, unless we understand them as being part of the dictates of the Corinthian society. Paul states that women "are commanded to be under obedience, as also saith the law." However, Divine laws do not ban women from speaking, but do mandate that all be obedient. Hence the law to not speak was a local law and it was women's obedience to the Lord's ordinances that enabled them to submit to the precepts at Corinth. However, for us, given that we understand that women held positions of leadership in Israel and prophecy foretells of them receiving God's Spirit to share the message of salvation, we identify Paul's instructions as a local requirement that should by no means prevail for us. It would make no sense and would contradict light which we will discuss now.

In other of his writings Paul presents that the duty of slaves (bondservants) is to obey their master. (Colossians 3:22) Does that mean that forever and ever there should always be slaves? Paul also declares the duty of men is to pray everywhere lifting their hands. (1 Timothy 2:8) How long has it been since you saw a man with lifted hands *all the time*? Does it mean men's prayers are of no avail, not valid because their hands are not lifted? Does that make any sense? Should we incorporate into our culture all of Paul's instructions for circumstances that were traditions? No. We must grasp the difference between God's will and man's culture of other times and places. Does it seem fair to stubbornly continue burdening women, yet we do not burden society imposing slavery or burden men demanding they continually lift their hands?

Paul comments in another of his epistles about "women who labored with me in the Gospel... whose names are in the Book of Life." (Philippians 4:3) Labored with him in the Gospel? How? Not speaking? "I will pour out my spirit... and your sons and your daughters shall prophesy." (Joel 2:28) Even God's angel at the tomb of Jesus committed to the women the responsibility of announcing the message of His resurrection, even to the other disciples of the Lord. (Matthew 28:1-7) And then, as the women started on their way to do just that, Jesus Himself appeared to them, confirmed the instructions of the angel by commanding *the women* to give to the rest of His disciples the news about His resurrection, and to also tell them to wait for Him in Galilee. (vs. 8-10)

Jesus could have very easily appeared directly to the disciples, but His command to the women confirms that there was no hidden agenda regarding them. In fact, at the cross Jesus first addressed His mother, then John the apostle. We learn in the rules of etiquette, that when we introduce two persons, the one of lesser rank is the one that should be introduced to the other person. An easy way to remember how to do that is to first address by name the person of greater standing or seniority, or position of wisdom or importance. (For example, "Mr. President, this is my neighbor." "Grandma, this is my boss.") When Jesus at the cross said, "Woman, behold thy son," and then addressed John, "behold thy mother," (John 19:26-27) He validated her dignity and His utter respect for women in general. In excruciating pain, nailed to a cross, Jesus magnified the Commandment, "Honor thy father and thy mother," (Exodus 20:12) by honoring her thus and making provisions for her well-being. Yet many, both males and females, are so into degrading women that they forget they have a mother whom they are indirectly dishonoring.

Further, because of women's status in the society of Jesus' time, it would have been more appropriate for a man to convey any news at all, his account of the events having more credence. Yet, by having women carry the news also serves to confirm that the resurrection of Jesus *is not* a fabricated hoax. That is because people who deceive try too hard to accommodate their presentation of lies as close to what is acceptable as possible. But by Jesus clearly directing women, and the writers giving an exact account of it, it served as further proof that there was nothing to hide. Hence this is yet an additional surety for us that the resurrection of Christ *is a fact* just as stated.

What, then, happened to Paul in Corinth regarding women? Women were good enough for God to have as judges and prophetesses, they were good enough for the angel at the tomb, and they were good enough for Jesus and those who wrote about His resurrection, but, apparently, they were not good enough for Paul. Did Paul turn wishy washy on us? Did he not have women labor with him in the Gospel? What is the Gospel? The Good News of a resurrected Savior which message women were the first to give; and fifty days later the Holy Spirit poured like refreshing rain on them also so they would continue in full force. It does not make sense that Paul would have women labor with him and then turn himself around when dealing with the church at Corinth. How do you explain that?

Another issue sheds light on Paul's actions. He *ordained* in all the churches *not* to circumcise anyone called while uncircumcised, but that he should remain uncircumcised. (1 Corinthians 7:17-20) In Christ, Paul said, all are the same, there is no Jew or Gentile. (Galatians 3:28) However, when Paul met Timothy, who was already a disciple, but uncircumcised, Paul wanted Timothy to go on with him, so he circumcised him because of the Jews who were in that region. (Acts 16:1-3) Contradiction? No. Paul ordained one way and then, at some point, acted contrary to his pronounced decree and conviction in order to not make waves in that specific region. In essence, neither being circumcised or uncircumcised was a sin. It was merely a painful inconvenience for the men.

Likewise, Paul demonstrated his conviction that women should labor in the Gospel by having them work alongside of him. In Christ, Paul said, all are the same, there is no male or female. (Galatians 3:28) Therefore, his statement at Corinth regarding women came as a result of a regional formality which was not of God's designation. In essence, neither speaking or not speaking was a sin. But since Corinth was a spiritually shaky region, Paul, as with the circumcision, esteemed it best to let the custom prevail in *that* church. He was not about to make any waves concerning it. He was making enough waves already with the tongues issue.

However, in no way did Paul, through these two issues, leave the example that when under pressure we may act against our own convictions, and that is not what I am saying here. We are called to glorify God and we do that obeying Him above obeying man. (Acts 4:19) But here Paul had the option of going either way and chose the route which brought no confrontation. Thus we observe that women were also good enough for Paul. In fact, we have him to thank for repeatedly condemning adultery and emphasizing that man is to be the husband of only one wife. (1 Corinthians 5:1; Galatians 5:19; 1 Timothy 3:2, 12; Titus 1:6) What a burden has been lifted for us ladies by Paul's words to that effect! They ushered in a healing process from the dictates that society had imposed upon the sacredness of marriage. Don't you love Paul? I do.

Unfortunately, "the law of the pendulum" sometimes may occur. Let me explain. When there is a way of life that needs to be addressed, at times some may go to the other extreme of their previous position, like a pendulum that is held to one side and when released will swing past the center. Likewise, since woman as "helper" for *her* man (one man, her husband) was turned by society into a "servant" of *any and all* men, then, upon correcting this, there may originate the problem of the pendulum swinging far onto the other side. Yet that imbalance does not mean the birth of a restoration for society was a mistake, for Jesus paved the way. It is sin that eclipses reason, and we should not allow ourselves to partake in the distortions of God's intentions by placing ourselves at either extreme.

We know that our sons, whatever age they may be, are to respect and honor their mother. Many of them, past the age when they become emancipated, out of love remain submissive to her. Before that age, however, they must be submissive as she has rights over them by being their protector, nurturer, mentor, defender and guide when they are toddlers or adolescents or are in early adulthood. But that does not mean that every single adult in the whole world has rights over her sons at all times, for only she does, given that she is the one that loves them best, safeguards them and fulfills their needs. All others would end up abusing them. I recall one day my boy came back home from the store very saddened. He had put a coin into a gum ball machine, but nothing came out of it. He asked the owner to please return the coin to him and the man told him to talk to the machine. I called him on the telephone and very calmly said, "Sir, do you realize that boy has a mother? My son will be there shortly." The man returned the money. It should have been a matter of common sense for him: Do not take advantage of a lion cub seemingly stranded.

In like manner, the submissiveness of *one* wife to *her* husband does not mean that every living male in the planet has any rights at all to rule over that one woman. Yet that is what has happened in many societies, and the world, deceived into having that right, uses it to trample over her spirit. Thus humanity has taken advantage of women's demeanor of mercy and has pushed many of them to the point of unbearable oppression and abuse. My husband, who spent a year in an African country, tells me he saw how some women there were burdened like animals. He recalls a man who had eight wives and they would work for him carrying heavy cases of beer on their head. The man guided them on the road using a stick as if they were a herd, keeping them in single file. They bore the title "wife" as a deceit, for in essence they were slaves.

In our society, some men, instead of using their position of justice to protect their wife—who is their physically weaker self—just as a mother protects her child of tender age, they are the ones who victimize her. And some women, who should reserve their endowment of mercy for those times when the family needs healing and nurturing because it is hurting due to intrusion, instead diverge their compassion by accepting and excusing whatever cruelty their husbands decide to inflict upon them and the family. Both behaviors are distortions of God's justice and mercy which each respectively represents and which united should reflect God's love. Thus Jesus, in the process of redeeming humankind from the oppression of sin, opened the way for all of us, including women, to commence to be free from the burdens we carry, whether self-inflicted or brought upon us by the dictates of society. Jesus came to free everyone from all tyranny imposed upon them, and Paul helped facilitate and advance God's work in that respect on behalf of women in particular by plainly addressing the duties of a husband, steering man to *also be submissive* in that he is to *submit his love* to only one woman. A wise woman gladly submits to such a man. (Ephesians 5:25-33)

This subject is so touchy that to this day there is strife concerning it. A brother from church told me he loves to mock his wife demanding of her, "You have to be obedient to me because the Bible says so!" And thereupon he cracked up laughing. "I tell her all the time to bother her and keep making fun of her until finally she gets sooooo mad. That's when I get a real kick out it." Ha, ha, ha some more from him. He was right in that Scripture states a woman is to obey her husband. But it also says that the husband is to love his wife. There are duties on both sides, like a contract. Yet in a contract, if one party fails to meet their end of the deal, the other party is free to not be bound by it. Jesus does not make fun of us, nor demands our obedience by force, but plainly just loves us and satisfies our needs; and we respond by obeying Him. However, a husband who demands obedience yet mistreats his wife, stirring her spirit to the point of robbing her of peace and joy, demonstrates by his behavior that he does not love her like Jesus loves the church. In essence, on the one hand he forfeits his rights and on the other he demands them. Contradiction is a giveaway characteristic of the old serpent.

Controversy regarding women exists to this day, in greater or lesser degree, in many regions. Sometimes more than others it is made manifest that the serpent's enmity for women since the beginning (Genesis 3:15) is alive and well. Discrimination, oppression, dishonor, debasement, degradation, offense, prejudice, despotism, tyranny, enslavement, use and abuse, insult, assault, battery, rape, dehumanization, humiliation, injustice, injury and all manner of wrong, including female circumcision, infidelity, abandonment, and rejection of her children, and the latter sometimes even by the very man who fathered them, Satan has lashed against women in particular.

Amazingly, many men, like Paul, find women good enough to work in the Gospel, while many women discriminate against themselves. The latter is more difficult to comprehend. But just as Gentiles were not to be troubled regarding the circumcision, just as we do not trouble men to lift their hands everywhere in prayer, and just as we are not to trouble society by imposing the reestablishment of slavery, so also we should not trouble women who are moved by the Holy Spirit to help in the finishing of the work. Burdening them so is a disservice to the Gospel, dishonors the command of resurrected Jesus to women to give the Good News, and perpetuates the hatred of the old serpent as if we were its little clones.

Should the helper be banned from helping in the eve of such a great need for laborers? Have not women, in many churches, always comprised the greater number of members, their monetary support even keeping it going, while they have not boasted about it or demanded any type of special recognition for it? Does not that fact alone in and of itself testify that their spirit is not into self glory? Have not the greatest number of converts in many churches come to the foot of the cross by the influence of a woman? If such has been the case when women have been laboring in the background, with the least of opportunities, does it not give a glimpse of how it would be when we finally acknowledge that the Holy Spirit can do with women whatever He wants? When will we accept the fact that God's Spirit is the One in control and that women are merely His instruments to use if and when He wants, the way He wants, and that we should not deter His purpose? Can we stop those women if their work is appointed by God? Of course not.

Spiritual sovereignty, as conveyed in chapter 2 herein,

diminished gradually from Eden to Jesus, and then it reverted. Now, at the culmination of its full reversal, women in drovers are answering God's call to ministry. Yet their full potential, when not ambushed, barricaded, or maimed, is at best tolerated with disdain as they are ushered to the rear of the Gospel bus. Hence the Lord's work is thus also blatantly mutilated.

And if it is, are we going to confront the Holy Spirit and fight against God Himself? (Acts 5:34-39) I am not referring here to any particular issue regarding women, save them preaching the Gospel. "When a great and decisive work is to be done, God chooses men and women to do this work, and it will feel the loss if the talents of both are not combined." (*Evangelism*, p. 469)

As we shall see in the last chapter, the world will experience another Pentecost and it is going to be BIG. In the first one, women preached. In the second one, the same will occur no matter how much we try to convince ourselves otherwise and even though we may resent seeing the engines warming up all around us getting ready for the grand finale as more and more women are convicted to enter the ministry. "Upon the servants and upon the handmaids in those days will I pour out my spirit," (Joel 2:29; Acts 2:19) and "your sons and your daughters shall prophesy." (Joel 2:28; Acts 2:18)

Please do not apply the old instruction of Paul to the Corinthians to block the Lord's work by those ladies who obviously give evidence that the Holy Spirit is guiding and using them as He moves them to work as preachers in God's vineyard. The entire chapter of 1 Corinthians 14 calls for banning from speaking in church those who should not speak: Women because of the custom at Corinth, and those with tongues not understood because of logical reasons. A contrast should be perceived. If it was improper for women to speak in church, then it would have been even more improper for any person to speak at all in church when his language could not be understood.

15

THE LATTER RAIN

The outpouring of the Holy Spirit promised for the last days is recognized by the term "the latter rain." Some who speak nonsensical tongues claim what they do is a manifestation of it. Let us consider the matter by first looking at certain facts surrounding the shower of the Holy Spirit on the day of Pentecost:

1. There were about 120 persons gathered who had the order to go into all the world and give the message of salvation. (Acts 1:12-15; Matthew 28:19-20)
2. They were behind locked doors at a perilous time in history fearing for their lives. (John 20:19)
3. They were all united in their belief as one man, and in prayer. (Acts 1:14; 2:1)
4. The Holy Spirit descended upon each of them and suffered them to go out and preach. (1 Corinthians 14:22; Acts 2)
5. As a result, about 3,000 persons were added that day to the group of believers in Christ. (Acts 2)

And that was only the beginning.

Peter attributed the outpouring of the Holy Spirit on that day to a promise given to the prophet Joel. (vs. 16) There we learn that the Spirit was promised to be given *twice.* (Joel 2:23, 28-29) God's Spirit is with us, but we are to look forward to the *second shower* of the Holy Spirit, to proclaim our message with the same vigor as the early disciples proclaimed theirs during the *first shower* of the Spirit.

Just as the Holy Spirit showered upon the scared flock to begin spreading Christianity, so shall the Holy Spirit shower upon the last generation to wrap-up the work of salvation. Joel characterized those two showers as the "former rain" and the "latter rain." (vs. 23) We should expect a manifestation of the Holy Spirit just as it took place on Pentecost, for it is promised, as some Bible versions present it, that it shall pour again "as of old" and "as first."

Prophet Jeremiah sheds light upon this subject saying: "Let us now fear the Lord our God, that giveth rain, both the former and the latter, in his season: he reserveth unto us the appointed weeks of the harvest." (Jeremiah 5:24) God has a time appointed for the shower of the Holy Spirit during a time which is Biblically recognized as the time of the *harvest*, that is, the harvest of souls, to commence and end the Christian era.

The first harvest: Jesus said, "Say not ye, There are yet four months, and then cometh harvest? behold, I say unto you, Lift up your eyes, and look on the fields; for they are white already to harvest." (John 4:35) Jesus was talking about reaping human hearts to gather them for the Kingdom of God. Jesus Himself was planting and spreading the seeds in men during three-and-a-half years of personal ministry. The seeds sprouted and grew, and when Jesus ascended to heaven, the Holy Spirit was poured out and the disciples gathered the harvest of mankind. Acting upon the Word of the Lord regarding the promise of the Holy Spirit, those who met behind locked doors on the day of Pentecost prayed for the former rain at its precise time, and as a result, Christianity would ultimately reach the whole world.

The last harvest: Can we know when the last harvest will take place? "And I looked, and behold a white cloud, and upon the cloud one sat like unto the Son of man, having on his head a golden crown, and in his hand a sharp sickle. And another angel came out of the temple, crying with a loud voice to him that sat on the cloud, Thrust in thy sickle, and reap: for the time is come for thee to reap; for the *harvest* of the earth is ripe." (Revelation 14:14-15)

Milestones leading to the last harvest: What event ushers-in the last harvest? The answer is found in the immediately preceding eight verses: Three angels give a unique message each, and then a voice from heaven speaks about those who work for the Lord. (vs. 6-13) The last harvest follows those eight verses. (vs. 14-15)

Angels are ministering spirits and our fellow servants. (Revelation 22:8-9) When we minister for the Lord proclaiming His message, we become heaven's ambassadors, hence God's three angels of Revelation 14. As such, we are the ones called to herald the final links in the chain of revelations given to mankind. We will discuss their proclamation below, but let us first analyze the statement made by the voice that immediately follows after them but immediately precedes the event of the last harvest.

That voice declares, "Blessed are the dead who die in the Lord from now on … they may rest from their labor, and their works do follow them." (vs. 13) Clearly, after the commencement of the three angels' message and before the last harvest, laborers will go to their rest. That means the three angels' message will be on-going past a generation or more. But as a way of encouragement to the laborers who go to their rest without getting to see the latter rain, this voice from heaven pronounces them blessed. Thus they know they do not work in vain; their labor will go on as others continue the proclamation up to the time of the promised upcoming harvest. Those who have studied extensively the three angels' messages know that said triple message began in the earlier part of the 19th century.

The first angel and Pentecost: The work of the first angel is presented in just two verses, (6-7) but *before* he begins to speak, it is made clear that he comes with "the everlasting Gospel to preach unto them that dwell on the earth." (vs. 6) Therefore, we learn that he arrives bringing with him the Good News about salvation in Christ Jesus resurrected, which is the everlasting Gospel. That was the message of Pentecost. That message has never ceased and cannot cease. It constitutes our firm foundation and thus it is confirmed that this first angel is in sync with the message of Pentecost. Then his own unique message begins and he speaks with a loud voice: "Fear God, and give glory to him: for the hour of his judgment is come: and worship him that made heaven, and earth, and the sea, and the fountains of waters." (vs. 7)

The first angel voices the proximity of God's judgment: *It has come!* Upon His return, Jesus will bring His reward with Him to give every man according to each man's work. (Revelation 22:12) That means that prior to His returning, a decision is made as to each man's recompense. Hence the first phase of the judgment, wherein is rendered the verdict which determines each man's eternal fate, takes place before Jesus returns. It is the outcome of the judgment which is delivered by Jesus as His reward to each man. Therefore, the investigative portion of the judgment does immediately precede the Second Coming, and since the Second Coming is very near, an angel, referred to as the first angel, is summonsed to announce that the judgment is at hand, has commenced. The timetable thus presented concurs with Daniel 7:10-14: "... the judgment was set, and the books were opened... yet their lives were prolonged for a season and a time ... one like the Son of Man ... was given him dominion... everlasting ... which shall not pass away...."

The first angel alerts us of the judgment and urges us to consider that it is imperative that the Lord Who created all things be worshiped. Thus far God had winked at man's shortcomings. "Therefore, having overlooked the time of ignorance, God is now declaring to men that all everywhere should repent because He has fixed a day in which He will judge the world in righteousness through a Man... having furnished proof to all men by raising Him from the dead." (Acts 17:30-31) Notice that in the preceding quote men are called to repent because a day of judgment has been set. Its text fits the first angel's message like a glove. Yes, a solemn era has begun and demands sobriety that all measure up to the full stature of the Law. Why? Because in order for one to be judged, there has to be a law that determines one guilty or not guilty. That law is the Ten Commandments. (Exodus 20:1-17) How do we know that?

The first angel proclaims God's title (Maker) and jurisdiction (heaven, earth and waters), and by so doing is in fact echoing the Fourth Commandment, (vs. 8-11) which is the only commandment that gives God's name, title and jurisdiction. Hence, by inference, this angel takes us back to Mt. Sinai and points to the complete stature of God's Law, for it is the only part of Scripture which the Lord spoke Himself and wrote for us with His own Finger. (Exodus 31:18) No one could be trusted with It. That detail alone speaks loud and clear of Its importance to God. Let us not treat the Original lightly. For something less than the Ten Commandments, Adam and Eve sinned, but the disobedience was the same and it cost the life of the Son of God. Shall we then treat the events at Mt. Sinai with disdain? Interestingly, the Second Commandment (*Ibid.*, 20:4-6) and the Fourth Commandment, (vs. 8-11, the forgotten one, the one which begins "remember") are the two longest requiring three and four verses respectively. Yet, both have been successfully attacked by Satan and pretended to be done away with. It was so prophesied in Daniel 7:25 that God's enemy would think of changing both times and law. In light of that prophecy, God's children should investigate whether the Ten Commandments have been, in fact, tampered with, and whether or not we are honoring a counterfeit law. All men who must come before a tribunal to be judged, review the laws applicable to the issue at hand in their case. Likewise, in light of the first angel's message, and the seriousness of our case in being tried in the eternal tribunal, we should do the same and look in the mirror of the *authentic* Ten Commandments which God spoke Himself and wrote Himself.

The second angel: He speaks with a normal voice and his

message comprises one verse only. He announces, "Babylon is fallen, is fallen." (Revelation 14:8)

The third angel: He also speaks with a loud voice like the first angel, but his message is the longest. It comprises four verses where, in the first three, he warns against worshiping that which opposes God, i.e., the beast, its image, mark, name and number, which is the sum of a blasphemy. (Revelation 13:1, 18)

Finally, in the verse which concludes the three angels' message, (Revelation 14:12) is defined the two characteristics which the Lord's last-day saints have: 1) they keep the Commandments of God; and 2) they have the faith *of* Jesus. Notice that having the gift of tongues is not an essential characteristic of God's people.

By ending his message with Jesus, the third angel completes the circle by bringing us back to the everlasting Gospel. Consequently, he also corroborates the message of Pentecost, and, by so doing, the three proclamations become tightened as one and anchored in Christ. Therefore, "order and discipline" or as Paul would say it, "order and decency" (1 Corinthians 14:40) in their plan of action becomes evident. Further, by the third angel defining the first characteristic of the saints as those who keep God's Commandments, he is confirming for us that we got it right when we concluded that the first angel was taking us back to Mt. Sinai so that God's Law, the Original, may be restored in us. And the last-day body of believers go a step further and also have the very same faith in God that Jesus had. It is the faith *of* Jesus that caused Him to keep God's Commandments such that He never sinned; and it is *that* faith *of* Jesus which will cause His people to do the same, thus His Character will be reproduced in them.

Messenger	Voice	Essence of message	Pattern
1st angel	Loud	Brings Gospel and exhorts to worship the Creator.	Light
2nd angel	Normal	"Babylon is fallen, is fallen."	Announcement
3rd angel	Loud	Alerts as to God's enemies.	Darkness

The three angels follow the pattern "light, announcement, darkness."

Problem. The darkness part of the message of the third angel is tough to share. Many will be offended and not view the messengers in a good light. For that reason, we may argue, "Isn't Jesus enough? Why create difficulty?" Why bother dealing with negative subjects and points of views differing from what is popular (like writing a book dissecting the gift of tongues)? Or, to the contrary, we may be zealous to face the consequences of any confrontation our message may bring, and eagerly we go forward letting the chips fall where they may. It seems as if we are in a predicament. We have a missive composed of different parts, some of which are good, some bad, and some ugly. If one worker concentrates on the good part according to his own ability, unfortunately, he may be criticized by another laborer who gives the ugly part and who, in turn, also gets blamed himself for his own section of the triple message.

What should be the solution? Should we pray for the Holy Spirit like on Pentecost so that we may still do the work? That is a good idea, but back then the believers were united as one man. We are not, so we have a dilemma. How could it be solved? Look at those angels. What do you see? Each kept to their message, but remained united. Shouldn't we do the same and join forces also? The brethren knowledgeable and eloquent in one area, keep to that part of the message, and so on, because the third angel does not say of the first, "he brings the Gospel and with him all is love, love, love, singing the world to sleep," and the first angel does not say of the third, "all he talks about is alarming news." Doesn't the triple message we are called to share reach the description of both extremes, of light and darkness, so that there is room for truth by all the laborers? Let us join hands and all go forward with the message of the hour. We are all needed. Every man's capability, talents and knowledge may play a part. As one in Christ, we may share the message of Pentecost *plus* the messages of those angels which will culminate in the latter rain.

As Christian ambassadors go to their rest, our enemy does not sleep but actively increases his efforts to deceive. Because he tried to duplicate the first coming of Christ prior to Jesus' birth, (Acts 5:34-39) it should not be a surprise that Satan pretends to also simulate another Pentecost. As a matter of fact, we will see that *that* is exactly what he does as time moves on. Therefore, another angel, very mighty, is summonsed to unite his strong voice with the voices of the three angels, and unmask the enemy. (Revelation 18:1-3) To facilitate our discussion of such grand event, let us refer to that latter angel as the "fourth angel." The chart below shows that this angel also follows the pattern "light, announcement, darkness," demonstrating he is finely in tune with the tri-fold message of God's end-time ambassadors.

Messenger	Voice	Essence of message	Pattern
4th angel	Cries mightily with strong voice	The earth is lightened with his glory.	Light
		"Babylon the great is fallen, is fallen."	Announcement
		Habitations of demons; foul spirits; and unclean and hateful birds.	Darkness

The fourth angel (Revelation 18) brings such glory that the earth is filled with light. (vs. 1) He then voices, "Babylon the great is fallen, is fallen." (vs. 2) Notice that the second angel had made reference to "Babylon" while the fourth angel makes reference to "Babylon the great." This tells us that something has happened to Babylon since the message of the second angel had first begun. As time has passed, Babylon has swollen into "the great" by successfully engulfing the whole world in darkness such that we merit the visit of a mighty angel. "Babylon," which origin we pick up at the Tower of Babel, is the root from which stems words like babble, confusion in speech, gibberish, nonsensical tongues. The fourth angel states that Babylon the great: 1) is become the habitation of devils; 2) the hold of every foul spirit; and 3) cage of every unclean and hateful bird. (vs. 2)

Habitation of devils: In Babylon there are men who are demon possessed. For examples of demon possession in Jesus' time, you may wish to look up Matthew 12:45 and Luke 11:26.

Hold of every foul spirit: In Babylon some may not necessarily be demon possessed, but their own spirit has become so defiled that they have become as demons. Terrorists and those who torture other humans fall into this category and are in essence demons in human flesh. Others who may seem passive may also fit the profile through sarcasm and jeering. Hate lives in their hearts so they do not need the devil to deceive them because they do a great job of it themselves, and by corrupting themselves, their own actions may tempt Satan to further tempt them. They are all the foul spirits in Babylon.

Cage of every unclean and hateful bird: We know that the Holy Spirit was present as a Dove when Jesus was baptized. (John 1:32). When the opposite, unclean and hateful birds, is introduced, then we know that a counterfeit of God's Spirit is at work and issues regarding the Holy Spirit are menacing. At the time John the Baptist saw God's Spirit as a Dove, the voice of the Father was heard with a clear message recognizing Jesus as His Son. In contrast, the voices in Babylon broadcast nonsensical tongues because it is the babble of its repulsive birds as if that was the latter rain. So cunning is the deception, that the more abracadabra borders in hocus pocus, the more convinced the people are that it is God's Spirit. But it is not. Not in vain was the warning by Jesus, "Will surely deceive, if possible, even the very elect." (Matthew 24:24) Thus the mighty *fourth* angel addresses the issue of the Holy Spirit falsified (impure birds) to open our eyes that we may behold our enemy's masquerade. In effect, Satan's agenda is spreading like wildfire via the false tongues and slain in the spirit movement, bringing the whole world under his unclean and hateful wings.

Besides the pattern of "light, announcement, darkness" followed by both the three angels united and the fourth angel individually, there is yet another detail which binds them. The three angels end their message by describing what constitutes the two characteristic of the saints, i.e., God's people. And the message of the fourth angel is immediately followed with the loud voice of another calling: "Come out of her, my people." (Revelation 18:4) Who obeys? The saints, God's people, those who yearn to keep the Commandments of God and have the faith *of* Jesus. Thus the Voice of One Divine culminates the work of the four angels. Through Moses, God summonsed His people to Mt. Sinai that they may hear His own Voice expressing His Character in the form of Ten Commandments; and now, via the four angels, God summonses His people to approach His Law. Then His own Voice speaks to their hearts and beckons them to come out of Babylon. "Come out of her, my people."

The Holy Spirit ushered in the work of evangelization as the early rain on Pentecost. As always, unless He impacts the hearts, all efforts are in vain. The most eloquent exposition of truth without the Holy Spirit offers no influence to the soul, while the simplest teaching bearing Its influence renders a transformation. Thus the

Divine Voice calling accelerates the work because the end of all things is at hand, and the Holy Spirit's presence in full force will wrap up the work *en masse* during the latter rain fast approaching.

Our duty thrusts us into promulgating the four angels' messages. That work involves the participation of all, both men *and* women. We know *that* because on Pentecost both male and female disciples were united as one man just as it was prophesied, (Joel 2:23, 28-29) and that same occurrence during the latter rain is inclusive in the prophecy. Further, angels are neither males nor females. Since we are the angels of Revelation, then it should not be considered whether we are male or female. All of us are messengers in Christ, in Whom also there are no males or females. (Galatians 3:28) Lastly, we could enumerate herein many more reasons for this to be so, but will only add this: Because the fourth angel cries mightily with a loud voice, his potency serves to magnify the proclamation of the other three when he joins them, and as their united voices intensify as they go forward, it is heard like a mighty great shout, a loud cry. Was there any other such powerful shout in the Bible? Yes, just before the walls of the city of Jericho collapsed. It is described that upon going around the city for the last time, the people shouted, in unison, a great shout (Joshua 6:5, 20) and the walls of Jericho fell flat. Who joined in their loud cry? Everyone, all the Israelites, men and women as one.

Each of us is called *individually* to be holy, reflecting Jesus. But it is not until godly men and godly women are *united* as one man that we will be a people *most* holy. The daily ritual in the sanctuary, which comprised the work of the priest in the Holy Place (Exodus 28:43, 29:36; Hebrews 7:27) serviced the individual. The yearly ceremony on the day of atonement and shadow of the judgment to come, comprised a work shifted onto the Most Holy Place (Exodus 30:10) and serviced the entire nation of Israel. Thus the Holy Place beckons us to be *holy individually* and the Most Holy Place beckon us to be *most holy united*. But if we are not united, we are still worshiping in the Holy Place. This is how we become united:

Paul and Barnabas parted ways (Acts 15:34-41) but continued spreading the Gospel, each according to their uniqueness and method. Therefore, though we may be broken off as independent ministries, we can still do the work according to our uniqueness, but united in spirit. It takes a miracle for each one of us to individually partake of the Divine Nature, but it takes a greater miracle for all of us to accept each other's singularity in love. Yet both miracles are God's intention to restore the world to how He first designed it, and God will not be mocked. (Galatians 6:7) It will happen. Who will cooperate with Him?

Jesus is in the second compartment, the Most Holy Place, of the heavenly sanctuary because the judgment is at hand. Some worship Him there while the rest of us who are not of one accord are still in the first compartment, the Holy Place. Unbeknownst to us, we worship Jesus without Him, for He has moved on to the Most Holy Place. Who will follow Him there? If we let the miracle of our surrender begin, we shall all stand and enter the Most Holy Place to be transformed into a most holy people, men and women ready to receive the latter rain. And when our voices in unison escalate into a loud cry, it is then that we shall hear the rumble coming from Babylon as its walls of errors fall flat. Are you ready to turn yourself in?

The world is spiritually asleep on the eve of a persecution. If a person is sleeping and the house has caught fire, what should be done? First, the person must be awakened with a vigorous shake. The hour is critical. The words must be alarming and precise. The third angel unveils the beast, its image, name and mark. His is an alarming wake up call. When the person awakens and is aware of the impending destruction, he seeks the door through which he may escape. Jesus is the door. (John 10:7-9) Since the first angel begins his message by having with him the everlasting Gospel, and the third angel leads us to God's Law and the faith of Jesus, we understand that we must be in sync with both the message of Mt. Sinai and the message of Pentecost if we want to be firmly anchored in Christ during God's judgment. It is a solemn communication which we have been entrusted with, and though there are ugly, troublesome and discouraging parts, we have been called to herald the last links in the revelation of God. Yet a pattern has been designed and left for us to follow: We begin with Christ, take cover in Him through the tempestuous portions of the message, in particular when the fourth angel joins the third angel, and then we return to Christ.

While Jesus planted the seed of his kingdom, the Jewish leaders sought civil authority to kill Him and used the excuse that they were securing peace for the nation. Similarly, while the messages of the three angels, along with the message of the fourth, mighty angel who exposes Satan masquerading as the Holy Spirit, are being proclaimed, the religious leaders of our day seek civil authority from all rulers of the earth, with the excuse of securing peace, and will ultimately end persecuting the small flock that is proclaiming those messages. The dragon is Satan himself, (Revelation 12:9) leader in the nonsensical tongues and slain in the spirit movement. The phenomenon is worldwide, spreading unconstrained, highly publicized, and within many denominations. No wonder a mighty angel is sent to assist the other three, to shake God's people out of its grasping hold and delusion!

Satan does not only manifest himself through a form of spiritualism which invokes the spirits of dead persons. Our enemy is too keen not to take us by surprise, and with all the strategy of evil, he has developed further forms of spiritualism, through throbbing music, chanting praises, frenzy outbursts, drugs, television, hypnosis, sensationalism, vain repetitions, falling unconscious, nonsensical tongues and anything that will be successful in controlling the souls with transitory emotions, and alluring the minds away from logic and reason. Aware that the end of all things is fast approaching, increased efforts have been prepared by Satan in order to divert the different minds, each by a custom-made deceit calibrated just for them. Ultimately, he desperately attempts to impersonate the Holy Spirit. Would our eyes open, we would behold the chameleon of evil disguising as leader in a vast and far-reaching movement which counts in the millions, and is promoted internationally on television. If there was such a thing as admiring evil, this enemy then is worthy of our admiration, but only to inspire us to seek refuge in God with constant fasting and prayer. Read again this paragraph and your mood will not be for party worship.

The Great Controversy points to the *two capital errors* of the Christian churches—the state of the dead and the Sabbath. However, regarding the angel of Revelation 18, it states that his message focuses on the "*additional* mention of the corruptions which have been entering the various organizations that constitute Babylon," (p. 603) since the message was first given by the second angel of Revelation 14. As a result of these additional corruptions, "the influence of evil angels will be felt in the churches." (*Ibid.*, p. 604)

What *additional* corruptions—and not the two capital errors—have entered the churches such that as a consequence demons control and manifest themselves in them? Are not some of those corruptions nonsensical tongues and being slain in the spirit? Nothing like it had been seen before in such great magnitude encompassing the whole world. No wonder that from the time the second angel's proclamation begun to the time the fourth angel joins in, "Babylon" grew to become "Babylon the great." The book goes on to state:

"Through the agency of spiritualism, miracles will be wrought, the sick will be healed, and many undeniable wonders will be performed. And as the spirits will profess faith in the Bible, and manifest respect for the institutions of the church, their work will be accepted as a manifestation of divine power." (*Ibid.*, p. 588) That is a perfect description of the miracles seen in the great movement of those that speak nonsensical tongues and practice being slain in the spirit. This new form of spiritualism, this new deception, described by the same book on pp. 554 and 588, and also *Desire of Ages*, p. 257, will be such that *Satan will appear in the character of "an angel of light."*

But wait a minute. Where in the Bible does Paul say that Satan manifests himself as an angel of light? In Corinth! (2 Corinthians 11:14) Notice the connection here. Paul makes us aware of the devil appearing as "an angel of light" in a discussion which deals with the problems of the Corinthians whose worship was contaminated by demonically speaking in tongues. Notice also the following statement: "And Satan, surrounded by evil angels, and *claiming to be God*, will work miracles of all kinds, to deceive, if possible, the very elect." (*3 Testimony Treasures*, p. 284)

Is not the Holy Spirit God? Is not Satan claiming to be the Holy Spirit? Satan disguises himself claiming to be the spirit of a dead person. Satan will disguise himself as Jesus imitating the Second Coming. BUT SATAN ALSO CREATES A DECEPTION DISGUISING HIMSELF AS THE HOLY SPIRIT. Thus we need to diligently study the issue of Satan impersonating the Holy Spirit as he did in Corinth. Demonic manifestations are all around us and promoted in the media as if from God. The time has come when we must believe God's Word over and above what we see with our eyes. John describes that he saw a woman sitting on top of a red beast; however, the angel who is explaining the vision tells him, "the waters where you see the woman is sitting." (Revelation 17:3, 15) But John did not see a woman sitting on waters, but on top of a red beast. How would we handle that? "Look here, Angel, I don't see any waters. I see a red beast." Or, "What are you talking about? What waters? I said I saw a red beast." Or maybe we would not argue with the angel, yet we would edit out of our writings what the angel said we saw which we did not see.

Brothers and sisters, the way John handled it is our guide. He did not argue with the angel, or even mention a discrepancy, and he did not edit out what the angel said. Perhaps John, because previously he had been shown a beast from the sea persecuting the saints (Revelation 13:1, 7) and now is shown a woman drinking their blood, (Revelation 17:6) understood that both were one and the same, and the origin of the woman is waters. But whatever the case may be, John's utter respect, honor and allegiance for the Lord's message is our guide for faith and trust in God's Word. John was looking at a woman whose name was "Babylon." (vs. 5) Babylon means confusion, in particular dealing with speech. When we see such confusion of doctrines accompanied by nonsensical tongues and supernatural stuff, and we will, because it is out there all around us and becoming a fashionable part of many Christian church services, then it becomes even more important to follow John's reaction and take God at His Word. Signs and wonder "will surely deceive, if possible, even the very elect." (Matthew 24:24)

A person who told me that by this my writing I am blaspheming the Holy Spirit and may have already committed the unpardonable sin, also added that if an angel appears with a message contrary to the writings of the Bible, that it is imperative that we follow the voice of that angel and not the Bible. However, her counsel contradicts the Word which says, "But even though we, or an angel from heaven, should preach to you a Gospel contrary to that which we have preached to you, let him be accursed. As we have said before, so I say again now, if any man is preaching to you a Gospel contrary to that which you received, let him be accursed." (Galatians 1:8-9) Clearly, there will be supernatural manifestations with instructions that will contradict the Bible. Perhaps they may not be supernatural, but doctrines and conclusions expressed via a preacher or lay person. Yet, if messages and beliefs presented contradict the Word, we are not to pay heed. Those messengers are not of the Lord, are accursed by God and, should we follow after them, we will suffer the same consequences as they. That is why it is necessary that we study Scripture for ourselves and get to know the Spirit of God ourselves.

"Nevertheless when the Son of man cometh, shall he find faith on the earth?" (Luke 18:8) The way that statement is phrased suggests that the answer is "no" because the whole world will be so totally deceived. Could that be possible? To show it is, below is a simple chart. There has never been a year zero.

Century	Years	Century	Years
1st	1-100	11th	1001-1100
2nd	101-200	12th	1101-1200
3rd	201-300	13th	1201-1300
4th	301-400	14th	1301-1400
5th	401-500	15th	1401-1500
6th	501-600	16th	1501-1600
7th	601-700	17th	1601-1700
8th	701-800	18th	1701-1800
9th	801-900	19th	1801-1900
10th	901-1000	20th	1901-2000

Each century represents 100 years. Hence the last year of the last century was year 2000 and the last day of that century was December 31, 2000. So why did we celebrate at midnight on December 31, 1999, the dawning of the 21st century as if it would begin the next day on January 1, 2000, when it was still one year away? Because the whole world was deceived in something as simple as arithmetic—not higher mathematics; basic arithmetic. In the late 1990's while the world prepared for the extravaganza celebration, a reputable magazine had an article about this error stating that it did not occur one hundred years earlier, for our ancestors rightly welcomed the dawning of the 20th century on January 1, 1901, not January 1, 1900. Yet the mistake kept brewing, and in our lifetime the real instant to celebrate the arrival of the 21st century and new millennium occurred uneventful, unnoticed and unmentioned as the special event that it was. Because we had already celebrated it *en grande* the previous year, the authentic moment for what should have been a great world-wide festivity, was observed just like another common new year. Such miscalculation and fallacy in basic arithmetic demonstrates that the whole world can be lead to uphold an error because, in fact, it did. Some knew that it was a mistake to celebrate one year ahead of its time as though it were the moment for the great milestone, but nonetheless went along with the flow. So it may be with many who, hearing this warning, still prefer to go with what is trendy, as if the actions of the majority are correct. And so it is that a multitude of Christians seem to be celebrating the latter rain, a false Pentecost, as if it were the real thing, or just because everybody does it. And then, when the genuine event is about to occur, is there going to be anyone of faith left to partake in it?

My brothers and sisters, we have a sacred missive from God to proclaim His messages clearly and to the point, for a spiritually asleep world is held captive in the arms of Satan. If we refuse to pay heed to the final messages, why would we receive power to preach during the next Pentecost if our starting point is shunning the very work God is calling His ambassadors to do? We need to know The Word well, we must beware of supernatural signs. John describes that he saw coming out of the beast, its image (false prophet), and Satan. (Revelation 16:13-14) three evil spirits like frogs, and it is not a coincidence that frogs are creatures that capture their prey with their tongues. Those frog-like spirits go to the kings of the earth seeking authority in their final war against God, for persecution is the culmination of Satan's plan to destroy those who proclaim the messages of the four angels. (Revelation

14 and 18) When the satanic trinity secures civil power, the wrath of Satan will be openly lashed against God's people, and they will realize that just like on Pentecost:

1. They are but a few in comparison to the persecuting powers.
2. They must remain behind locked doors because of fear for their own lives.
3. Because they all agree upon their beliefs and message, they are sealed as one man.
4. They will pray for the Holy Spirit's final, grand outpouring, and God's Spirit will shower upon them as the second refreshing heavenly rain. Their fears will vanish and they will head out to proclaim their message in full force and vigor.
5. As a result, their numbers will multiply daily as the last harvest of humans unites to Christ.

When that occurs, the Holy Spirit will provide whatever means His people need to accomplish the final spread of the Gospel very quickly during perilous times, for soon Jesus will appear in the clouds of heaven to take us home, and we shall meet the Lord in the air. (1 Thessalonians 4:16-17) Now is the time to prepare for the accomplishment of the grand work entrusted to us by God. The end-time disciples who will partake in the final proclamation, from their hometown to the ends of the earth, will eloquently articulate in every language known to man the message of salvation in Jesus, our resurrected Savior, and our need to have His faith and keep God's Ten Commandments as He did. The grace of God will be with those messengers, and as they speak, their words will bear the anointing of divine authority, for the Holy Spirit will give to their words power and, of course, *meaning*.

Amen

Testimony

In 1980 I began studying the subject of tongues. When I clearly saw the findings presented herein, I needed to write my conclusions for the sake of my children who were young at that time, because, if something would happen to me, I wanted them to be able to read the results of my study when they grew up.

At that time there were no personal computers yet and I purchased a modest but new electric typewriter. Within a few hours of use, it stopped working, so I exchanged it for another of better quality, but the same thing happened. The third typewriter, still more expensive, also gave me a few hours of use. For the fourth typewriter I paid even more and purchased maintenance insurance. Soon enough I had to send it out for repairs and shortly after it was returned it demised for good. There seemed no way I could print out the results of my study.

At about that time word-processors invaded the market. I recorded my study in a floppy disc, but when I went to print the computer gave a message that the data was lost and unrecoverable. The second and third discs went bad also. When I typed once again the study right into the hard drive and went to print, I got the message: "CANNOT PRINT." Nothing like that happened with other documents. It took much prayer to finally print a simple version of this study.

Then in church I heard an elder present a lecture about God's Spirit. Afterwards I approached him asking if at some time I may speak with him for an hour or so. I did not tell him what it was about, but he invited me to go to his home at three o'clock that afternoon. We sat across from each other in the dining room at a large round table. His wife and children were in their bedrooms napping. Thereupon I proceeding to share my findings for the first time. However, I spoke for about two hours and he did not say a word during all that time, just looked at me attentively, without nodding approval or disapproval. That was strange. When I concluded, he said in amazement, "Now I understand!" That was even more strange. What was going on? "When you told me you wished to speak to me," he said, "I assumed you were going to ask me for guidance in some problem and immediately began to pray that God would give me discernment that I may advice you sensibly. But as I was praying, the Holy Spirit spoke to me one single word ordering me, "Listen," that is all. And I did not pray more about the matter, but wondered why I would have to listen to your problem, yet not counsel you. Now I understand." He invited me to return the following week at the same time, and his wife and three children were sitting around the table. He invited me to join them and when he sat down said, "Now I would like you to teach my family what you taught me last week." I did. That is how I began to share the results of my research.

Thereafter, the church board voted unanimously that I should present to the church a study on this subject. However, the day before the board met I had a dental appointment to have a root canal done. The dentist injected the anesthetic and waited, but there was no effect. So he gave me a second shot. Soon I felt my legs becoming numb, and I became so drowsy that I realized I was not going to be able to stand up and walk without assistance. Mumbling the words, I asked the dentist if it was possible that an anesthetic shot in my gums would numb my legs. He turned pale and immediately ordered oxygen, then tilted the dental chair so that my head would be lower than my feet while I was wearing the mask placed over my mouth and nose. I overheard two dentists commenting that my heartbeat had dropped from 86 to 55 because the anesthesia went into a blood vessel when injected, and in turn traveled to my heart. My heart, instead of my gums, was numbing from the first shot, and that was why blood was not reaching my legs. A circle of persons formed around me. Some persons have died in a dental chair due to this type of accident. It does not happen often, but it happens. I waited praying, then I felt my gums get numb. I told the doctors and everyone sighed in relief. Consequently, I shared this study in church.

Months later I was scheduled to speak in another county. Three days before, I lost my sense of direction for about an hour. When I thought I had turned left, I had actually turned right and found myself away from where I wanted to go. I thank God I was walking and not driving. That afternoon I had to rest and was dizzy in bed for two days unable to go to work. With some sisters praying for me, I was able to be of sound mind as I spoke in the church where I was invited to present this study.

Teresita Pérez

RIGHTEOUS BY FAITH

Author: Teresita Pérez

Man was created by God,
his flesh formed from earth's clay.
Thus he's dust, bound to be carnal;
and passions would rule his way.

But the seed of faith declares war
against the flesh and seeks God,
just like seeds, when they are planted,
struggle against the sod.

Faith is a gift from God,
a seed buried for a while
that stubbornly fights the ground.
The battles of faith are trials.

Each tree grows after its kind.
Likewise, through his talents, man
patiently works in God's ministry
when faith abides in the heart.

The leaves are for nature's medicine,
remedies to be used in healing,
just like kindly deeds and mercy
give the heart a happy feeling.

Then the tree gives forth its flowers,
and faith bouquets of obedience,
for nature displays the pattern
of heaven's science with patience.

The flower suffers a change
and, voilà, a fruit is formed,
and so it is that obedience
likewise into fruits transforms.

The fruits represent God's holiness
which eternal life encloses.
(Romans 6:22)
And the perfect cycle closes.

It continually repeats
into more fruits and more seeds,
yielding thus a greater faith
that's neverending indeed.

Living faith looks up to heaven
like a tree out in the forest
with its branches reaching upwards
giving God eternal glory.

It's the trials that make it stronger.
Through mercy it yields more leaves
that cool the weary and tearful,
and offers him shade and peace.

Righteous By Faith

When the man of faith obeys,
then beautiful flowers bloom,
roses are multiplied
and all may breath their perfume.

Then, at last, the man is righteous.
The fruits can now be seen.
They're worthy of admiration.
From sin he has been redeemed.

Those fruits of faith that are holy,
for our communion were formed.
God's character is in them.
By faith we may be transformed.

But not by faith that is dead
like a seed that doesn't sprout.
But obedient, kind, like Jesus.
That's what faith is all about.

Like oil that is used to soften,
in the early spring rain falls
softening the ground, and helping
the little seed to grow tall.

The harvest will yield much fruit,
gathered at the season's end,
if upon the grown up plant
then showers the latter rain.

Likewise, I wish to bear fruit
and meet all of human needs,
that mankind delight in finding
there's plenty of food to eat.

That is why I pray to God
that in me His early rain,
my character soften, sweeten,
that trials may not be in vain.

I am that tender, young plant
that needs to conquer the sod
through showers, the Oil of grace:
the Holy Spirit of God.

And then, at the end of the work
that He bids to do so fine,
transforming me unto Himself,
to a character divine,

I pray for the latter rain,
cascades of water receiving,
for it's His Spirit in me
even as in the beginning.

Then it is that I shall be
shelter, food, and all that's graceful;
and it would have been worth the while
all the trials, for which I'm grateful.

Righteous By Faith

It's from seed to many fruits,
from faith onto righteousness,
each step under grace, with power.
By God's Spirit's how I'm blessed.

Like a tree I seek the heavens,
and shall reach up all my days,
even after the Lord's verdict:
"I find you righteous by faith."

We invite you to view the complete
selection of titles we publish at:

www.TEACHServices.com

Scan with your mobile
device to go directly
to our website.

Please write or email us your praises, reactions, or
thoughts about this or any other book we publish at:

P.O. Box 954
Ringgold, GA 30736

info@TEACHServices.com

TEACH Services, Inc., titles may be purchased in bulk for
educational, business, fund-raising, or sales promotional use.
For information, please e-mail:

BulkSales@TEACHServices.com

Finally, if you are interested in seeing
your own book in print, please contact us at

publishing@TEACHServices.com

We would be happy to review your manuscript for free.